AFTER WOUNDED KNEE

John Vance Lauderdale, ca. 1888. Photograph courtesy of the Beinecke Rare Book and Manuscript Library, Yale University.

AFTER WOUNDED KNEE

Correspondence of Major and Surgeon John Vance
Lauderdale while Serving with the Army Occupying
the Pine Ridge Indian Reservation, 1890-1891

Edited and with an introduction by
Jerry Green

Michigan State University Press
East Lansing

All Michigan State University Press books are produced on paper which meets the
requirements of American National Standard of Information Sciences—Permanence of
paper for printed materials ANSI Z39.48-1984.

Michigan State University Press
East Lansing, Michigan 48823-5202

03 02 01 00 99 98 97 96   1 2 3 4 5 6 7 8 9

Library of Congress Cataloging-in-Publication Data
Lauderdale, John Vance.
    After Wounded Knee/Jerry Green
        p. cm.
    "Correspondence of major and surgeon John Vance Lauderdale while serving with
the army occupying the Pine Ridge Indian Reservation. 1890-1891."
    Includes bibliographical references and index.
    ISBN 0-87013-405-1 (alk. paper)
    1. Wounded Knee Massacre, S.D., 1890—Personal narratives. 2. Lauderdale, John
Vance—Correspondence. 3. Lauderdale, John Vance—Diaries. 4. Physicians—United
States—Correspondence. 5. United States. Army Medical Department History. 6. Teton
Indians—Medical care. 7. Pine Ridge Indian Reservation (S.D.)—History. I. Green,
Jerry, 1946- . II. Title.
E83.89.L38 1995
($ #.'' ?—dc20
    95-35471   CIP

To
My Sunshine,
My Love,
My Life,
My Gail.

Contents

Foreword

In March 1994 James M. McPherson came to town. The Pulitzer-Prize-winning historian and author of the grand Civil War narrative, *Battle Cry of Freedom* spoke one evening to a rapt Lincoln, Nebraska, audience of academics, history buffs, and students. The subject of Dr. McPherson's lecture was the motivations of the nineteenth-century warriors for the Blue and Gray, what they fought for and why (see his *What They Fought For, 1861-1865*, [Baton Rouge: Louisiana State University Press, 1994]). Describing his research in progress, he detailed his methods and offered some initial conclusions while effortlessly illuminating the master historian's art and craft.

What struck this listener was the (seemingly) severe restriction that McPherson had placed on his data, the raw material from which he had constructed his argument. From the vast Civil War documentation—a body of work that America's Indian war studies can never challenge—he used only contemporary first-person accounts, the diaries of participants and their letters to intimates, accounts that largely were never meant for outside eyes. This historian, therefore, had factored out the self-serving reminiscence, the grossly embellished newspaper story, and the politic official report. What remained for his examination was the work of a host of authors exposing their innermost thoughts, beliefs, prejudices, and motivations, a literature that possessed a remarkable potential for creating new insights on a familiar subject.

Move, if you will, from the Civil War army to its scaled-down descendant of the 1890s, to a cultural struggle between the United States and the Lakota people, and to a letter writer who initially states, "I shall not be able to give you any information of the Sioux War till I get farther West." This line serves as a cautious prelude to a particular set of correspondence authored by Dr. John V. Lauderdale, a veteran army surgeon sent west in January 1891, preserved by the Beinecke Rare Book and Manuscript Library of Yale University and prepared herewith for publication by Jerry Green.

Although from a different time and place, the Lauderdale letters as uncensored, contemporary historical documents apparently meet the stringent criteria demanded by McPherson, and are sources treasured by all historians. Unlike the scorned newspaper reporters "who are writing for their bread and spin long yarns for their readers" (4 January), Dr. Lauderdale shared his observations and opinions on the "Sioux War" with the closest of his family members, in particular his wife Joe and sister Frank. His letters apparently reached no wider readership during his lifetime, nor did he rewrite them later to fit a later generation's biases or an older man's needs.

Contrasting this to the voluminous literature of the Lakota Ghost Dance, the Wounded Knee Massacre, and the U. S. Army's Sioux Campaign during the winter of 1890-91, one soon sees Dr. Lauderdale as a most singular source. Much has been written on these topics, an almost constant stream of words since the 29 December 1890, slaughter of Chief Big Foot and his people in South Dakota. For a while, Wounded Knee took center stage in the nation's attention. Covered by the national press, at least two dozen journalists from newspapers across the country reported on the happenings on Pine Ridge Reservation. Officials representing the civil and military arms of the federal government, the imposing bureaucracies of the departments of Interior and War, created enormous paper trails of the events, simultaneously saying much but revealing little.

Eyewitnesses to the carnage along Wounded Knee Creek and to other examples of bungling by the decision-makers also kept records, and for the past century their words in the form of published reminiscences have served as fodder for the debate on what really occurred. Much of the literature on the events of that awful winter and their consequences, both first person and secondary accounts, is understandably self-serving or slanted and receives uncritical acceptance or immediate rejection depending on how well it fits preconceived notions of the particular theorist or advocate. As Lauderdale himself wrote, "Everyone has some axe to grind, some benefit to derive from the situation" (24 February).

Herein lies the value of this contribution to the literature of Indian-white relations in the American West, specifically as it relates to its most violent manifestation, the Wounded Knee Massacre, and, as Lauderdale termed it, "the closing out of this war business" (18 January). To a subject for which thousands of pages of text exist has now come a new source, a new voice, one that leapfrogs so many others in its day-by-day accounting of the aftermath of Wounded Knee, as well as its context. We receive frank appraisals of fellow officers, sketches of notable personalities, and complaints of office politics, views one scarcely encounters in other documents and which are even rarer when one considers they came from an insider, an army medical professional assigned to that campaign. The private correspondence of John Lauderdale affords today's readers the uncommon luxury of peering over a stranger's shoulder and garnering a voyeuristic glimpse at his life. In so chronicling himself, the good doctor fills his final prescription—allowing us, as he termed it, to "get order out of confusion" (22 January)—and thereby enhancing our understanding of his times.

R. Eli Paul
Nebraska State Historical Society
Lincoln, Nebraska

Acknowledgments

This volume could not have been produced without the resources of many splendid libraries, archives, and other repositories of historical records. These institutions, however splendid, cannot stand alone. The people staffing such organizations make all the difference to the researcher.

I cannot praise the following people highly enough. George Miles, curator of the Western American Collection, Beinecke Rare Book and Manuscript Library, Yale University, and his staff, especially Lori Misura and Stephen Jones; Heather Munro of the Lilly Library, Indiana University. Kitty Deernose of the Archives of the Little Big Horn National Battlefield; Dr. Richard J. Sommers and David Keoug of the United States Army Military History Institute, Carlisle Barracks; William Lind and Michael Meir of the Military Reference Office, National Archives and Record Administration, Washington, D.C.; Robert Lee of Sturgus, South Dakota; Ted Hamilton of Oglala Lakota College; Mrs. Alan Carrick, great-greatniece of Dr. John R. Von Hoff; Sanford Betz, great-grandson of Hospital Steward Appel; James Flavin great-greatnephew of Clarence G. Morledge and John Carter, Richard Jensen, and Martha Vestecka-Miller of the Nebraska State Historical Society.

Other institutions that allowed access to their facilities are: the Agricultural Engineering Department, South Dakota State University; the Lee Library, Brigham Young University; the Library of Congress; the National Archives and Record Administration, Washington, D.C.; The National Climatic Data Center; the National Archives and Record Administration, regional branches in Kansas City and Atlanta; the National

Anthropological Archives, Smithsonian Institution; the National Museum of Health and Medicine, Armed Forces Institute of Pathology, Walter Reed Hospital; the Frederic Remington Art Museum; the National Library of Medicine;. the Denver Public Library, Western History Collections; the South Dakota State Historical Society; the Kansas State Historical Society; and the Colorado Historical Society.

My appreciation goes to Ms. Belita Dreaden and Ms. Lorraine Hulings for their proofreading skills, time and patience.

I would be remiss if I did not mention Fred Bohm and his splendid editorial staff at the Michigan State University Press. My gratitude to Fred for his confidence and support, and to the staff, especially Julie Loehr, Michael Brooks, Kristen Lare, and Kristine Blakeslee. Their editorial skills and tireless effort added much needed polish to my research.

Special thanks are due to some remarkably special people. R. Eli Paul, of the Nebraska State Historical Society in Lincoln, Nebraska. He first made me aware of the Lauderdale papers, and it was at his urging that I undertook the editing of this volume. Without his support, editorial advice, and encouragement this work would not exist. Dr. and Mrs. James W. Wengert of Omaha, Nebraska offered me their friendship and hospitality. And Doc. gave me his encouragement and shared his research materials. By providing his expert insight and knowledge on the frontier army and the medical department, as well as the technical aspects of nineteenth century medicine, he made my job much easier. Mike Her-Many-Horses of Wounded Knee, South Dakota, provided help, guidance, and support in reviewing my manuscript, and made suggestions for changes and corrections. Most importantly I am grateful for the acceptance and friendship I received from him and his wonderful family.

This book or anything else I may ever undertake would not be possible were it not for the patience, support, encouragement, understanding, and love of my beautiful wife, Gail. She has endured many long, lonely hours while I was away on research trips or just in the back room "playing with my book." With much gratitude and undying love, I dedicate this work to her.

Editor's Notes

The journals and correspondence of John Vance Lauderdale are preserved in the Western Americana Collection of the Beinecke Rare Book and Manuscript Library at Yale University, New Haven, Connecticut. The collection totals twenty one boxes of material, covering the period 1838-1931. The preponderance of material spans the years 1852-1916.

The letters presented here are his entire correspondence from 1 January 1891 to 3 March 1891. No evidence could be found of a journal. Most of the letters are written on 7^1/$_2$" by 10" lined paper folded to form four pages per letter. For a few letters he used 8" by 9" lined paper folded length wise to form four pages. The letters written en route to Pine Ridge used both sides of a 3" by 6" pocket-size tablet. He used mostly black ink, although he sometimes used pencil. Lauderdale wrote in a steady, even hand, and most letters are surprisingly legible, considering the circumstances under which they were written.

In retirement Lauderdale collected his letters and mounted them on a heavy backing paper using tape. Over the years the adhesive from the tape has bled through the paper, causing the ink to run and some of the pages to stick together. This is particularly true of the pocket-size tablets that contained his correspondence from 1 January 1891 to 6 January 1891. Therefore, some portions of these letters are missing. This method of mounting has done little damage to the remaining letters.

Lauderdale's words are presented as written in his own hand. In rare cases, where text has been omitted due to illegibility, ellipsis points have been inserted. In cases where one word is illegible, because of damage from the tape or otherwise impossible to read or decipher, I have inserted words that logically fit the idea of the sentence. These insertions are indicated by enclosed brackets.

Lauderdale frequently misspelled names and incorrectly identified people. When a mistake is suspected, my correction appears in brackets. All parentheses and underlining are Lauderdale's, and although spelling and some punctuation errors have been corrected, no attempt has been made to change word tense or usage.

Lauderdale's words are presented exactly as he wrote them, and some words or phrases may be offensive to certain people or groups. I have kept these words and phrases strictly for historical considerations and regret any discomfort they may cause the reader.

Chapter One

Background

The world of John Vance Lauderdale was that of an army doctor during the last third of the nineteenth century. During his career, he witnessed significant changes in medical practices and army life. He also provided to posterity a view of the daily life in the American West through the writings contained in his journals and letters.

The majority of his writings cover his career in the military, which began during the American Civil War and lasted until he retired in 1896. His views and opinions were freely expressed in letters to his wife and sister, private letters that tend to present a reliable depiction of events with more perception than official reports or stories written for publication in the mass media.

With the exception of his Civil War letters[1] Lauderdale's writing about the events that he witnessed and had intimate knowledge of are virtually unknown. This volume focuses on his letters from Pine Ridge Reservation during the so-called "Great Sioux War of 1890-1891."

John Vance Lauderdale

Lauderdale was born on 13 November 1832, in Sparta, New York, the eldest of the six children of Walter E. and Mary A. (Vance) Lauderdale. He was closest to his sister, Frances Helen, two years his junior, whom he affectionately called "Frank." The vast majority of his correspondence was addressed to her. When John was two years of age, the family relocated to

Geneseo, New York, where he received his primary education. His course of study was literary, classical, and scientific.[2]

His father was a physician, a vocation he did not encourage his son to pursue, due in part to low pay and long hours. In the spring of 1851, Lauderdale went to New York City to learn the apothecary trade, and found his first job at the firm of Rushton Clark and Company. He did not enjoy his position as clerk in the drug store, finding the six day work week nearly unbearable. He soon found employment at the wholesale drug firm of Boyd and Paul.

Living in New York allowed him many opportunities not available in his rural home town. His activities were that of any pious young man alone in an urban environment. He absorbed as much of the city's culture as he could afford, although low wages and social status limited his social life. These limitations, however, did not prevent him from attending frequent free lectures in places such as Clinton Hall and free readings provided by the library. A devoutly religious man, like his father, he joined the New Brick Presbyterian Church in 1853. To satisfy his natural curiosity, he constantly read and spent his free time sightseeing. Natural history and geology became his ardent pastimes, interests that he would follow for the rest of his life.

In August 1855 Lauderdale moved to Cleveland, Ohio, to work in yet another drugstore. Here his interest in geology blossomed, as nearby coal fields provided many opportunities to explore for fossils. In February 1857 the natural scientist in him emerged, when he was invited to join the Williams College expedition to the Florida Keys. A loan from his father enabled him to join the expedition from February through April.

He returned to Geneseo in early spring 1858 to enter medical practice with his father. That fall and the following winter he attended the University of New York to pursue the formal study of medicine. In the fall of 1859, he interrupted his studies when the trustees of the Temple Hill Academy in Geneseo urged him to take charge of their natural science department. He accepted their offer on the condition that the position not permanently interrupt his studies. He held this position for two years, and was able to accumulate enough money to finance his second, and final term of Medical School. He returned to New York University Medical College in the fall of 1861 and graduated in March 1862.

After graduation, Lauderdale accepted a position on the staff of Bellevue Hospital in New York City as a junior assistant surgeon. The Civil

War delayed his reporting for hospital duties until the following October. Instead of reporting to Bellevue, however, the young doctor signed on with the U.S. Army as a contract surgeon. Contract surgeons were civilian doctors under contract to the army, usually for a period of one year. This move was at the urging of his brother Willis, a telegraph operator in St. Louis. Willis assured him that he could learn more surgery in one year in the Army than in a lifetime of medical practice in New York. As a bonus he would be paid at the same rate as a second lieutenant, $100 per month. He obtained permission to delay reporting for his staff appointment at Bellevue.

Assigned to the Department of Tennessee, he served on the hospital ship *D. A. January* under the medical command of Alexander Hoff.[3] The steamer transported over 3,000 wounded soldiers, both Union and Confederate, during the five months Lauderdale served aboard her. He was disappointed that most of the casualties treated were due to illness and did not require the surgical treatment that Lauderdale had hoped to practice. Because knowledge of bacteria and aseptic surgery was limited at that time, many battlefield casualties died of what are considered minor wounds by modern medical standards. Disease, not wounds, caused the vast majority of casualties, with the sick suffering from diarrhea, dysentery, typhoid, typhus, and malaria. Young Lauderdale saw his share of pain and suffering.

Upon his release from the army at the end of his contract period, Lauderdale returned to New York City in October 1862. His staff duty at Bellevue Hospital lasted another eighteen months, with four of those months spent at the Blackwood Island facility. Fulfilling his obligation in the spring of 1864, Lauderdale contracted again with the U.S. Army. Appointed an acting assistant surgeon, he received orders to report to Utah Territory in the Department of the Pacific, for ultimate assignment at Fort Bridger, in the present state of Wyoming. He spent the next two years at Bridger.

His perspectives of the world emerged during these years. He believed that recently-freed blacks should have the right to vote. In a letter to his sister Frank dated 27 April 1866, he stated his enlightened beliefs that blacks should enjoy civil liberties, had the right to an education, and should not be subject to flogging. Fort Bridger also offered Lauderdale his first contact with Native Americans. His initial views were stereotypical of the time. In a letter to his sister Frank dated January 1865 when he wrote:

If they won't work like other people they had better be exterminated. They are nothing but a nuisance and an obstruction to civilization. I do not believe in Indian Reservations and Indian exclusiveness the only way [is] to bring them to civilization and train them to duty and good behavior at once . . . Let them know that they too must earn their bread by the sweat of their brows instead of eking out a miserable existence by hunting . . . Every Indian village or tribe is a nest of inequity and ought to be broken up.

On 4 February 1865, he wrote to Frank, "Hang the Indian they are a nuisance." The Indians Lauderdale spoke of were, of course, those still free to roam and hunt as they had done for generations.

He revealed this attitude again on 26 May 1866, he described the cutting down of telegraph poles and removal of the line by Indians. His indignation revealed itself when he stated:

. . . every red-skin must be killed from off the face of the plains before we can be free from their molestations. They are of no earthly good and the sooner they are swept from the land the better for civilization . . . I do not think they can be turned and made good law abiding citizens any more than coyotes can be used for shepherd dogs.

Later encounters with native people confined to reservations and at the mercy of corrupt Indian agents profoundly altered Lauderdale's attitude.

His attitude was typical of many whites on the frontier. They surmised that European Americans were advancing civilization by bringing their culture westward and that their philosophy, technology, and religion would civilize Native Americans. Whites could not accept the fact that Indians had their own religion, culture, and civilization. As time passed, however, Lauderdale's basic attitude toward Indian people changed, even though his ethnocentric or at times racist notions would persist.

According to Lauderdale, the Indians' only hope for their future lay in their ability to "work and earn a living like white folks." As most reformers and Indian rights activists of the late nineteenth century, Lauderdale expected Native Americans to adopt the lifestyle of the white farmer virtually overnight. These well-meaning reformers lost sight of reality, forgetting that it took their European ancestors many generations to evolve into what they considered civilized society. These high-minded reformers expected Indians to reach the same levels, in both agricultural skill and cultural values, within a single generation but did not consider the impact on the Indians' culture or day-to-day life.

Duty in the west brought Lauderdale into contact with another group with whom he was unfamiliar, the Mormons. A devout Presbyterian, his comments on the Mormons leave little doubt about his feelings on polygamy. He thought it was as evil an institution as slavery and considered the Mormons an impious people.

By early 1866, his future still appeared uncertain, he applied for commission in the regular Army. He was commissioned in December 1866 and remained in New York City examining recruits until June 1867, when he was appointed assistant surgeon with the rank of lieutenant. His rank elevated his social status and allowed more time and money to enjoy the cultural attractions the city had to offer. He spent leisure time at the theater, lectures, and museums, and proximity to his hometown provided many occasions to visit his family. In June 1867, the Lyceum of Natural History elected him a member.

In the summer of 1867, he received orders to report to the Department of California. He arrived in California in August 1867 after a journey via the Isthmus of Panama; the journey was one of his most cherished memories. He wrote of the adventure that lasted over three weeks and of his desire to return as an amateur naturalist. He wanted more time to study the flora and fauna of the jungle, a desire that he would not fulfill until the twilight of his years when he returned and saw the "Big Ditch."

In California he was assigned to the Presidio of San Francisco. Again he was able to enjoy the culture of a large city, with its diverse population. Ceremonies in Chinatown made a lasting impression on him. He also relished the social life of an army officer, but his enjoyment was short-lived: in April 1868 he received orders to Fort Yuma, Arizona, where he remained for the next three and one-half years. His chief complaints about the post was the lack of a chaplain and the lack of piety among the officers and men.

Fort Yuma offered his first encounter with Indian life on a reservation. His opinion of Indians changed as he realized the neglect and suffering these people endured. As a devout Christian, he was very sympathetic to their plight and often suggested better treatment for these government wards. He

**Captain and Assistant Surgeon John Vance Lauderdale ca. 1874.
Photograph courtesy of the Beinecke Rare Book and Manuscript Library,
Yale University.**

shared the concerns of many of the organizations formed to support the rights of Indians. Sympathetic to the Indian predicament, one of their goals of these groups was to eliminate the corruption that was rampant within the very same government agencies that were charged with the welfare of those on the reservations.

Most agents and other officials of the Bureau of Indian Affairs were political appointees. The spoils system was deeply entrenched within the federal government, and on most reservations the agent and his staff changed with each change of the administration in Washington. The men appointed as agents were rarely qualified for the position. Agency traders and contractors in collusion with the agent frequently profited at the expense of the Indians.[4]

In agreement with popular opinion of the time, Lauderdale believed that the best way to eliminate corruption would be to give the army control of Indian affairs. That plan was not without its flaws, however.

He wrote in September of 1868, "The question of turning the poor Indian over to the War Dept. The plan in the main is a good one, but there are many Army men who may be in command of Indian countries [sic] who will not be a benefit to the Indian, rather an injury." Undoubtedly he was speaking of the "Indian haters" and those officers who partook of "old John Barleycorn" in excess.

His journal cites those men who " . . . like all the Army loves his whiskey too well." Alcoholism was a major problem in the army in general and in the West in particular. Some posts reported alcoholism rates extraordinarily high even by contemporary standards.[5] Lauderdale recognized the problem of military alcoholism before it became generally acknowledged by the army, once again far in advance of his time. Alcoholism, he said, was the " . . . internal fires that are gradually decimating the Army."

Promotion to the rank of captain came in May 1870. In June 1872 he was transferred from frontier duty to New York and served at Forts Wood, Hamilton, and Wadsworth in New York Harbor. He relished the cultural and social amenities of the city even more than his previous tours because he knew he would soon be back in the West. After short tours in Fort Adams, Rhode Island, and Fort Leavenworth, Kansas, Lauderdale spent the next four years in New Mexico Territory.

His first critical written report of Indian agent corruption came during his tour at Fort Leavenworth. In a newspaper article he wrote on 22 August

1874, he discussed many of his views on Indian affairs. His main concern was the army takeover of the Bureau of Indian Affairs, as proposed by General Phillip H. Sheridan. He also discussed the right of the Indian people to live in peace with their neighbors. Specifically, he favored the philosophy that the Indians should be provided for by the government until such time as they could be taught the skills necessary to provide for themselves. He believed earlier than many that the Indians did not possess agricultural or mechanical skills and were at the mercy of unscrupulous whites. Some of these unethical white men would and did, cheat the Indians out of everything they possessed.

Lauderdale also advocated "all the privileges of citizenship" for the Indians when they reached a position to exercise the role. He expounded the idea of each tribe having its own reservation, to which even those Indians opposed to such an idea would be forcibly confined. The reservations would be governed by the army until the Indians were ready to assume that role for themselves. This would require the use of troops in the place of a police force. Keeping with popular opinion of the day, he stated that the best way to control them was through fear and punishment, not by feeding and coaxing. Lauderdale believed that the only way to control a hostile native population was through the use of "the breech loading rifle in the hands of a soldier."

The second point of his article dealt with the corruption of the present Indian agents. He believed that responsibility for the welfare of so many people was a formidable task even for an honest agent, and the corrupt agent had no accountability. The Indian had no recourse except through the very agent responsible for generating the poor conditions.

Lauderdale attacked the policy of making "solemn treaties with ignorant and immoral Indians who have little conception of right and wrong." He compared the Indian to the residents of Blackwell's Island, a facility in New York for convicts that also included a shelter for the indigent, insane, and violent. Ultimately, he strongly advocated the Christianizing of the Indian. These attitudes would change even more by 1891, when the letters contained in this volume were written.

In 1874 at Fort Wingate, Lauderdale had the opportunity to study Zuni culture and archeology, and conduct some amateur anthropological fieldwork, scientific activities that were of great interest to him. While at Fort Wingate he also first encountered the "colored troops," or "Buffalo Soldiers," of the Ninth U.S. Cavalry. This crack regiment won his immediate respect and admiration. These were the same soldiers who, fifteen years later, were among the first troops to arrive at Pine Ridge. The Ninth Cavalry rescued the Seventh Cavalry on White Clay Creek the day after the Wounded Knee massacre and saved them from a fate similar to Custer's at the Little Big Horn. Lauderdale resented the segregationist treatment of the black soldiers in the army. The medical department was required to keep specific accounts of their diseases, and the separation of medical records by race was a practice he found degrading to the troops and a waste of his time.

While stationed at Fort Defiance, New Mexico, in 1875, he addressed the subject of corrupt Indian agents in another newspaper article. In an undated newspaper article found in his collection entitled "From our correspondent in New Mexico," he wrote of fraud and dishonesty by the former Indian agent, William F. M. Arny, who had been withholding goods sent to him for the Indians under his care, later selling them on the open market for his personal profit. Lauderdale was contemptuous of the system that allowed dishonest agents to profit at the expense of the Indians.

The years between 1879 and 1881 were spent in the South at posts that included Mount Vernon Barracks Alabama; Newport Barracks, Kentucky; McPherson Barracks, Georgia; and Jackson Barracks, New Orleans. Lauderdale's time in the deep South solidified his sympathetic attitude toward blacks. In at least one case he provided funds to a black woman W.A.C. Caldwell, to help her with her education, enabling her to obtain a teaching certificate. He also occasionally attended services at various black churches.

His interest in science continued and led to many experiments with the latest inventions. In one such adventure, while at Mount Vernon Barracks in 1879 he connected his quarters to the post hospital with one of Alexander Graham Bell's new telephones. He repeated this experiment at several other posts where he served.

During his tour in Alabama, Lauderdale married Josephine Lane of Brooklyn, New York, a woman he forever called "Joe." His letters to Frank and his father discussing the upcoming wedding reflected an excitement not found in any of his other correspondence. Married on 29 June 1880, the couple honeymooned in Europe for several months prior to Lauderdale reporting for duty at Fort McPherson, Georgia, near Atlanta.

On 6 March 1882, Lauderdale received orders to report to the Department of Dakota. Except for relatively short tours of temporary duty, Joe, and later the children, would accompany him on all of his assignments. The couple reported to Fort Sully, twenty-three miles north of the present-day capital of Pierre, South Dakota, on the Missouri River. While there, Lauderdale was able to pursue his interest in geology, spending time in the Bad Lands west of Sully exploring and digging for fossils. He also enjoyed taking weather observations. He expressed as much fascination over the extremely cold temperatures of the Dakota winters as he had over the extreme heat of Arizona.

Fort Sully was situated deep in the heart of Sioux country. It was one of the posts that encircled the Great Sioux Reservation, providing Lauderdale insight about the native peoples. He watched as they drew their meager rations on issue day, which came but once a month, and observed the poor quality of the annuity goods such as coats, blankets, and pots and pans.

The four-year tour at Fort Sully was marred by the death of the couple's first child, Frances Helen Lauderdale, named after his favorite sister Frank. The baby had thick brown hair and brown eyes just like Frank, according to the proud father's letter to the baby's aunt. Little Helen, as she was called by her parents, died fewer than four weeks after her birth in August 1885. The death of this child was perhaps the most emotional experience of his life. His letters to Frank revealed much more pain and hurt than he intended to show. Notwithstanding his own heartache, he voiced the anguish felt by Joe without divulging specific details. Some weeks later Joe wrote to Frank describing the infant's last days and revealed a closeness between the two "sisters," as they called each other.

Lauderdale's journal entries were most revealing. "This has been a sad and gloomy day for this household. Our little Helen that has been the hope and joy of us both went to sleep last night about midnight never to wake . . . Joe has been quite broken in spirit today."

The infant was placed in a casket, hand-made by a soldier on the post, with the interior lining made by some of Joe's friends. After a simple service, Lauderdale, refusing assistance, lifted the casket and carried it to the cemetery himself.

Cautious following the death of their first child, the Lauderdales journeyed to the Lane home in Brooklyn for the birth of their second daughter,

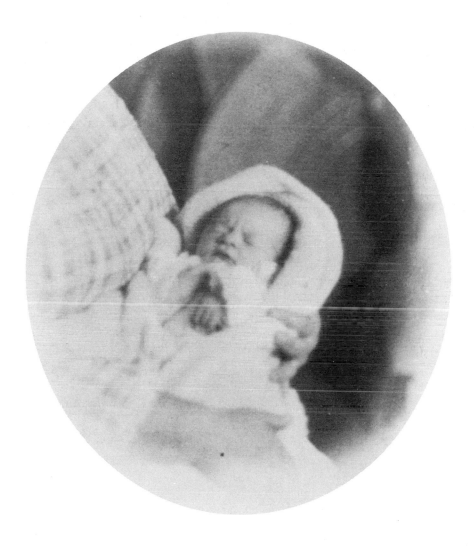

**Frances Helen Lauderdale, 1885. Photograph courtesy of the Beinecke
Rare Book and Manuscript Library, Yale University.**

Marjorie Lane Lauderdale, born 30 September 1886. Orders to go to Texas came in December of that year.

The next four years spent at Fort Concho, Fort Clark, and Fort Davis in Texas were uneventful, with the exception of a lawsuit that jeopardized his career. Lauderdale was accused of not paying a debt that he felt was unjust. His commanding officer, Colonel M. A. Cochrane, was preparing to court-martial him, but Capt. Frank D. Baldwin, who would soon become his commanding officer, intervened on Lauderdale's behalf and had him reinstated. Baldwin and Lauderdale became lifelong friends, as did their families. Lauderdale also met and befriended other officers he encountered again at Pine Ridge in the winter of 1891. In July 1888, he was appointed surgeon with the rank of major.

Much rejoicing accompanied the birth of the Lauderdales' son, John Vance Lauderdale, on Thanksgiving Day 1889. Little Marjorie showed much excitement and Aunt Frank wrote a letter to young Vance, as he was called. Less than six months after Vance's birth, orders came for their dream post, Fort Ontario, New York, where they arrived in May 1890. The Doctor was assigned temporary duty at Fort Wayne, near Detroit for a few weeks in July, 1890. Numerous activities such as concerts, church functions, and the nearness of family made the next four years among the most enjoyable of the doctor's career.

The Medical Department of the Army

It is evident from his journal entries for December 1890 that Lauderdale had been keeping abreast of the news from the West. On 29 December 1890, as the tragedy of Wounded Knee Creek unfolded half a continent away, Major and Surgeon John Vance Lauderdale once again received orders to report to a western station, this time to the Pine Ridge Agency on the Oglala Sioux Reservation in South Dakota.

Events of the summer and fall of 1890 caused great alarm to settlers in Nebraska and South Dakota living near the Sioux Indian reservations. The fear spread and got out of control, and eventually troops were sent to quell what many thought was an uprising in the making. This was an opportunity for the army to attempt its first mass deployment of troops since the Civil War. The generals could test new weapons, equipment, and tactics, and the medical department could test its ability to summon medical personnel and hospital equipment from around the country in the event of casualties.

Soon after the Civil War, the federal armies were disbanded. The regular army shrank to its peacetime strength of 25,000 men[6] and to its previous state of service in small, isolated posts, primarily on the western frontier. The army's medical department also returned to a peacetime status. Headed by a surgeon general, who had overall control of the medical department, each of the army's geographical departments was assigned a medical director. Individual posts had hospitals, which were manned by post surgeons and hospital stewards, and larger posts might have one or more assistant surgeons. A small number of enlisted men drawn from the ranks of the units assigned to the post provided a work force to assist the doctor and steward. The medical department, due to its small size and limited manpower, was unable to provide much more than routine care. Contract surgeons were widely used to augment the inadequate number of medical personnel.[7]

During the days following the Civil War, the medical department operated much as it had in the past, but this system proved inadequate. Line soldiers, from cavalry and infantry units assigned to each post, were used to assist the surgeons in the operation of the hospital. They could be retained for months on hospital duty and were thus unable to serve in their primary roles in their operating units. The men on temporary loan from the front line were not trained in medical matters, and the quality of care provided to the sick and wounded, never considered good, declined further. Nonetheless, many medical officers expended every effort to bring about needed improvements in the operation of the medical department. In time they succeeded.

In 1893 Major Charles Smart, considered one of the brightest officers in the medical corps, noted that,

> provisions for first-aid to the injured has been the subject of earnest study by medical officers for several years back. The War of Rebellion [as the Civil War was often called] gave the Army Medical Department a large experience which had not been altogether lost by lapse of years, for although most of those who were personally engaged on the great battlefields had dropped from the ranks of active workers, many of them had placed their views on record or impressed them on younger officers who have served with them as subordinates.[8]

Dr. Smart further noted that there were two obstacles that delayed progress of the medical department. The first was, ". . . the quarter century of peace and prosperity enjoyed by our country since the close of the Civil War has been so beset with Indian hostilities that the medical department has had little opportunity of keeping itself in proper training."[9] The second was the failure of that vague power known in military parlance as "superior authority" to provide suitable personnel for hospital duty. Smart's comments on this subject were also eloquently blunt: "The commanding officer disliked to lose good soldiers from the ranks, but readily spared any man who was broken down, valueless from innate stupidity, or worse than worthless from dissipation."[10]

Of the medical officers, Smart declared,

> the men he could get, not the men whom he wanted, were those that the medical officer had to prepare for duties of giving first-aid to the injured; and afterward, when by dint of care and assiduous personal attention to their physical and moral well-being he had repaired the broken constitution, awakened the intelligence, uprooted the evil habits, and endowed these men with possibilities of future worth, they were probably transferred [back] to the ranks and the hospital provided with substitutes as worthless as those that had originally been sent. After laboring in vain to build a hospital system with such bricks, the most enthusiastic medical officer generally subsided into a state of resignation.[11]

During this period between the Civil War and the war with Spain there was comparative inactivity in the army with the exception of the Indian Wars, which involved a relatively small number of troops. This same era is noted, however, for being one of the most dynamic periods in history for the advancement of medical science and technology. The germ theory of disease was developed, and much was learned about the prevention of intestinal diseases in large populations, although this knowledge proved incomplete when it came to implementing it among troops in the field.[12]

Several years later army medical historian Colonel Charles Lynch noted:

> During the period under discussion the discoveries in regard to pathogenic microorganisms had been utilized most extensively in surgery, with the

result that the technique of clean surgery had been perfected. In military surgery, though the first-aid packet had been developed, improvement in the technique of preventing infection in extensive lesions had not progressed far. This was equally true of similar surgical lesions occurring in civil life. Many years were yet to pass before wounds attended with great destruction of tissue were to fall under surgical control. [13]

Despite the obstacles, the period between the two major wars was marked by major accomplishments in the medical department, accomplishments that would have a lasting impact on the regular army. In 1885, directives were issued to medical officers to perform monthly sanitary inspections of their posts and report the results to Washington, forwarded by the commanding officers. The effect of the requirement was that by 1886 the sick rates were low, despite the continued lack of bathing facilities and sewerage and the continued use of unsanitary privies. [14]

The annual report of 1888 showed further advances in sanitation. The surgeon at Fort Sill wrote:

Three years ago [when he joined the station] the men had only rough pillows and bed sacks, filled with the coarsest kind of hay, for bedding. Now they have good wire spring mattresses and hair pillows, sheets and pillow slips, all of which they highly appreciate. Then the squad room walls and bedding were infested with vermin to a most annoying degree: now there are no complaints and no occasion for any. Then the only bathing facilities during cold weather consisted of a wash-tub taken into the mess room: now there are very good bath and lavatory accommodations, properly heated in the winter, so that the men can bathe at any time, which they do frequently. Then the water supply was scanty and of doubtful character: now it is abundant and of the best quality. [15]

The organization of a hospital corps and its influence on the subsequent history of the medical department must not be overlooked. Prior to the formation of the corps, it was impossible, during peacetime to make any real preparations for war. The medical department had no men to train, which put limitations on the training of the medical officers, who learned from teaching. In addition, it was virtually impossible to form efficient and cohesive medical teams within the medical units with soldiers temporarily on loan from the regiments stationed at that particular post.[16] This corps consisted of men enlisted exclusively for duty in the medical department, replacing the system of detailed cooks, bakers, nurses, and civilian personnel.[17] The formation of the Hospital Corps was authorized by several acts of Congress, which set the total number of men, their qualifications, and their rate of pay.

In 1882 the 47th Congress set down the qualifications for hospital stewards. Men appointed as stewards must be

> . . . experienced druggists or apothecaries, with a practical knowledge of pharmacy and minor surgery, such as the application of bandages, the dressing of wounds, the extraction of teeth, the application of leeches, as well as a good working knowledge of nursing and the preparation of food for the sick; also, in view of the responsible duties devolving on hospital stewards, often being left in charge of the medical department and in the care of the sick at a military post for days and sometimes weeks, during the temporary absence or sickness of the post-surgeon. . . .[18]

Congress waited until 1886 to address the subject of pay for the stewards. These men had petitioned the surgeon general of the army for "pay and allowances in a position commensurate with the important nature of their duties." Stewards were also given the same rank status and privilege of a non-commissioned officer.[19] The number of stewards was dictated by Senate Bill S.1119, passed during the second session of the 49th Congress on 19 January 1887. This bill authorized stewards to be permanently assigned to the medical department and not counted as a part of the army's total strength, as previously authorized by Congress. This bill also limited each post to one steward and required an examination by a board of one or more medical officers. Qualifications similar to those for stewards were defined for a class of acting hospital stewards and privates of the Hospital Corps.[20]

By 1888 the organization of this new hospital corps was nearly complete. Only a small number of vacancies remained to be filled. The corps was now able to participate in field maneuvers with regular troops, although the only routine military work required of the medical department was hospital corps drill. In this drill, certain men of the line regiments were added to serve as company litter bearers. The drill consisted of

marching with and without litters, dressing wounds, picking up and carry-
ing patients, and loading ambulances.

In 1889 Dr. John Van R. Hoff, considered one of the creators of the field
hospital system, established a school of instruction for members of the
Hospital Corps at Fort Riley, Kansas. Drawing on knowledge acquired in
part from European army sanitation practices, Hoff was instrumental in
establishing both the field hospital and hospital corps concepts.[21] In addition, medical officers began to learn to command men and to become familiar with army business methods. On some posts the medical officer was
responsible for procuring his medical supplies as well as routine supplies for
the day-to-day operations of the post hospital. Knowledge of overall medical
organization in war was required, and this knowledge was formally tested
before promotions.[22]

By 1890, when Charles Sutherland assumed the office of surgeon general,
the medical department was considered progressive. There was a growing
interest in sanitation, the practice of antisepsis was so common that it neither
required nor received special mention, and officers were submitting numerous reports upon professional subjects.[23]

The Situation on the Sioux Reservations in Dakota

Events on the Sioux reservations brought together, on the plains of the
Dakotas, the largest force of the U.S. Army since the Civil War. This deployment was also the last major mobilization of the army against Native
Americans. Improvements in communications and transportation provided
the army with a superiority it had never before enjoyed in its confrontations.
Generals could test new weapons, equipment and tactics under field conditions. The railroad made possible the rapid movement of troops when and
where they were needed. Telegraph lines and heliographs made communica-
tion between commanders almost instantaneous.

This large force also required the support of the medical department and
hospital corps. Medical officers, stewards, acting stewards, and privates of
the hospital corps from across the country received orders to proceed to the
trouble spots. Medical officers had to be recalled from leaves of absence to
fill vacancies. Among the medical department personnel sent to South
Dakota was Major and Surgeon John Vance Lauderdale. Lauderdale was sent

from the relative peace of his dream post of Fort Ontario, near the town of Oswego, New York, to join the force occupying Pine Ridge Agency, South Dakota, on 29 December 1890. That same day well over 260 Lakota, mostly women and children, met their death in what would become known as the Wounded Knee massacre.

After the Wounded Knee massacre, the first armed confrontation between the army and the Lakota during this disturbance, fear and apprehension escalated on both sides. No one knew for certain what would happen next. The army feared an all-out assault on the agency. The possibility of bands of hostile Lakota attacking nearby settlers was considered real. The Lakota, surrounded by this large force of troops, became increasingly alarmed. They feared an attack on their villages and camps by the army, as had happened so many times in the past. This is the atmosphere Lauderdale found upon his arrival at Pine Ridge on 3 January 1891. With the subsequent surrender of the "hostiles," the army disbanded this large force. Lauderdale remained at his post until most of the troops returned to their permanent stations, a billet he found increasingly onerous.

Events of the summer and fall of 1890 brought alarm to settlers living near the Sioux reservations in South Dakota. Fear spread out of control, eventually causing the army to send troops to quell what many thought to be an uprising in the making. The situation which resulted has been labeled many things: The Great Sioux War of 1890-1891; The Ghost Dance War; The Sioux Uprising; or The Messiah Craze War. It could, however, be labeled nothing more than a civil disturbance put down by armed U.S. soldiers.

The Lakota people then living on the reservations had from sheer desperation turned to a new religion, looking for hope in their dismal existence. When ordered to stop the practice of this new religion, they refused. When they asked for the same religious freedom granted by the constitution of the whites, they were perceived as hostile and war-like, even though they did not possess a standing army and were without the means to offer armerd resistance, especially in the winter.

The Teton (Lakota) division of the Sioux Nation was formed by the confederation of seven tribes: Oglala, Brule, Hunkpapa, Miniconjou, Sans Arc, Two Kettle, and Blackfeet. The Lakotas were among the largest and strongest tribes living on the Great Plains. In spite of war, disease, and loss of game and land caused by white migration, their number exceeded 25,000 in 1890.[24]

The treaty negotiated at the end of the Red Cloud War of 1868 designated the western half of South Dakota for the Lakota reservation. The right to hunt on the land north of the North Platte and the Republican Fork of the Smoky Hill River, their traditional hunting lands, as reserved exclusively for the Lakota.[25] The Indians believed that they had retained the exclusive right to hunt within the limits of their old range, which included parts of present day Montana, Wyoming, and North Dakota (see fig. 1).

The Bureau of Indian Affairs appointed agents to oversee the reservations and issue rations and annuity goods. The government promised to set up schools and provide physicians and resident farmers to teach agricultural skills. Military posts were also built around these lands, effectively encircling them, and railroad companies obtained permission to lay track across Lakota hunting lands. The coming of the railroad brought emigrants and hunters. The buffalo on which all Plains Indians depended for most of their necessities were exterminated. The discovery of gold in the Black Hills within the reservation brought an influx of people to that beloved land, which by treaty belonged exclusively to the Lakota.

The Great Sioux War of 1876, which included the famous Battle of Little Big Horn, resulted in another pact. The treaty of 1876 reduced the reservation further, including the loss to the Lakota of their beloved Black Hills (see fig. 2). In 1889, after several attempts, the government succeeded in further reducing the great Sioux reservation by more than 9 million acres.[26] The "surplus" Indian lands were needed to accommodate a growing influx of European immigrants. The mining operations in the Black Hills required access to the markets east of the Missouri, and railroad access from the eastern half of the state was needed to accommodate cattlemen, farmers and freighters. All of these special interests put pressure on the government for the cession of Sioux lands that effectively cut the state in half.

The need for a rail line linking the eastern part of South Dakota to the Black Hills and for more land for the growing number of Dakota settlers brought about the formation of a commission to negotiate further concessions from the Lakota. The Sioux Land Agreement of 1889 divided the great reservation into smaller agencies. These reservations were Standing Rock, Cheyenne River, Lower Brule, Crow Creek, Pine Ridge, and Rosebud (see fig. 3). These remaining reservation lands were arid, sandy, and not suited to

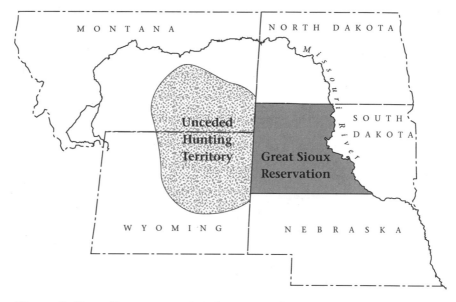

Figure 1. Sioux Reservation after the treaty of 1868.

Figure 2. Sioux Reservation after the treaty of 1876.

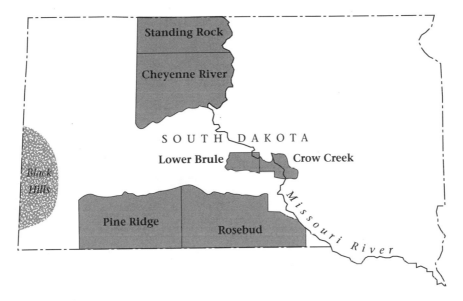

Figure 3. Sioux Reservation after the Land Agreement of 1889.

agriculture. Droughts commonly resulted in failures of the meager crops that were raised.[27]

Prolonged drought had began in central South Dakota in 1886.[28] Many white farmers gave up any hope of ever farming the arid land and moved on.[29] Some opted to use the land to graze livestock, as country was better suited for grazing than farming. The Lakota did not have that option. They were forced to attempt to raise crops in spite of the government's refusal to provide the full allowances of seed, agricultural tools, oxen, or cows. The Lakotas' food rations were reduced to the point of causing widespread hunger and, in certain cases, starvation. Rations intended to last for a specific time period were inadequate for less than two-thirds of that time.[30]

The late 1880s brought a series of catastrophes to the Lakota people living on the reservation. In addition to crop failures due to drought, an outbreak of deadly black-leg disease among the Lakotas' cattle took a heavy toll. In 1889 and 1890 epidemics of la grippe, measles, and whooping cough caused suffering and death of many Lakotas.[31] The situation grew worse after the government reduced rations.

Perhaps the most serious blow was the reduction of rations in 1890. After the Lakotas signed the Land Agreement of 1889 surrendering over nine million acres of their land, congress cut their rations further, although the Lakotas had been assured by the commission that negotiated the agreement that their rations would not be reduced. For example, the beef ration was cut on the Rosebud reservation by 2 million pounds and on Pine Ridge by 1 million pounds. Similar reductions took place at the other agencies.[32]

The Land Agreement of 1889 and the events surrounding it caused conflicts among the Lakota. The schism between the progressive and traditionalist Lakota widened. The progressive Lakota were those who willingly followed government policy. The traditionalists consistently opposed any further concessions to the government.

The Interior Department recognized that lack of food was one of the causes of dissatisfaction among the Lakota. On 1 December 1890 Secretary of the Interior John W. Noble ordered the commissioner of Indian Affairs to issue rations, "even if you have to draw on supplies intended to extend throughout the fiscal year, or on appropriations or funds unusual for this purpose."[33] Secretary Noble's response came only after he received complaints from army officials occupying the reservation concerning the lack of adequate food and the general condition of the Lakotas.[34]

Another source of discontent among the Lakota was the annuity goods due them under the treaty, which were issued late if at all. The issues of winter clothing and equipment due on 1 August were not issued until mid-or late winter. As late as 12 December 1890, the annuity goods were issued to the Lakota at the Cheyenne River Reservation. The goods had remained in a Pierre, South Dakota, warehouse due to lack of transportation: one report stated that they were waiting for the river to freeze to transport the goods rather than utilizing the ferry.[35] This would allow more profit for the civilian contractors, but caused great suffering among the Lakotas.

The removal of their children to attend school in far-off Carlisle, Pennsylvania, instead of providing day schools or boarding schools on the reservations also caused dissatisfaction among many Lakotas. When their children returned to the reservation from school, jobs were unavailable.[36] In short the reduction of the Lakotas' lands brought about by questionable actions and methods of the Sioux Land Commission of 1889, along with the effects of previous agreements generated much ill will toward the whites.

At the same time as the Lakotas' world appeared to be disintegrating, rumors of a messiah in the far west began to filter into the reservations. The subject of the rumors was a Paiute medicine man by the name of Wovoka who lived near Walker Lake, Nevada. This man, known to local whites as Jack Wilson, had experienced a vision, which led to the formation of a new religion, one which said the white man would disappear from the country. The prophecies also called for the resurrection of all the Indians' dead ancestors, the return of the buffalo and other game animals that had been destroyed by the whites, and the reestablishment of the dominance of the Indian people.[37]

In the fall of 1889, delegations were sent from several of the Lakota reservations to investigate this messiah firsthand. They returned with the good news that all they had heard was true.[38] The second coming of God to earth would benefit the red man, not the white.

In the spring of 1890 another delegation left for Nevada to confirm what they had heard from the first group. These men learned the tenets of this new religion from Wovoka and became devoted to its doctrine. The men of this delegation became leaders of the new religion among the Lakotas.[39] This new religion, became known by its most publicized ceremony, the Ghost Dance, which was its principal expression of worship. The Lakota people saw the religion as a source of new hope, and some embraced it with exhilaration. The majority, however, did not subscribe to the doctrine and joined the camps of Ghost Dancers only after the appearance of troops on the reservation.[40]

Contrary to the beliefs of the whites, the doctrine of this new religion was not warlike. Wovoka preached peace and he directed his followers to go to work, send their children to school, and wait peacefully for the prophecies to come true. As the summer of 1890 passed, the religion and the dancing associated with it spread throughout the various western reservations.[41]

To nearby settlers in Nebraska and South Dakota, and some less experienced Indian agents, however, the new religion caused great alarm. As the dancing spread, so did fear among the settlers. Out of ignorance of their Lakota neighbors, they thought any Indian dance was a war dance. Fear that the Lakota would stage an uprising to drive the whites from their former lands swept the frontier. These fears were totally unfounded, for, as noted, the doctrine of the religion advocated peace.[42] As the number of dancers increased, however, so did the pressure on the Indian agents to stop the dancing.

Daniel F. Royer, a physician and former druggist without prior experience dealing with Indians, was named agent at Pine Ridge in October 1890, a political appointment arranged by Senator R. F. Pettigrew of South Dakota.[43] On 3 October 1890, shortly after assuming his duties, Royer received orders to stop the Ghost Dance on Pine Ridge.[44] Unable to do so, Royer called for troops to stop the dancing as early as 12 October 1890.[45] On 11 November 1890, Royer issued a warrant for the arrest of an Oglala Lakota named Little who had been accused of stealing beef. Little resisted arrest and was subsequently rescued by a group of fellow Ghost Dancers.[46] Two days later Royer wrote to the commissioner of Indian affairs, "We have no protection and are at the mercy of these crazy dancers." Perain P. Palmer, the agent at Cheyenne River, also requested aid.[47]

Royer was afraid of his charges; the Lakota named him "Young Man Afraid of His Indians."[48] A more experienced agent could have kept the situation under control, and his behavior was reported as erratic and unreliable.[49] Much blame can be placed on Royer's lack of experience and fear of the Indians leading to the armed intervention on the reservation.[50] A possible explanation for Royer's behavior is that he was using drugs during his short term as Pine Ridge Agent. Some years later he lost his license to practice medicine due to substance abuse.[51]

Agents were instructed by the commissioner of Indian affairs to supply the names of the Ghost Dance leaders for possible arrest.[52] Agent Reynolds on the Rosebud submitted the names of twenty-one men. McLaughlin, the long-time agent on Standing Rock, requested only Sitting Bull and five others be arrested and removed. Palmer, the agent on Cheyenne River, wanted Chiefs Hump and Big Foot, and three others removed. Agent Dixon at Crow Creek reported no problems.[53] Agent Royer at Pine Ridge submitted a list of sixty-four men to be arrested, and added that that might not be enough.[54] He later said "60 or 70 should be arrested to insure peace here."[55]

Many people who had been among the Indians and knew the Lakota knew there was no reason for concern. Dr. V. T. McGillycuddy, the former agent at Pine Ridge reservation, reported, "As for the ghost dance, too much attention has been paid to it."[56] His belief was that when the spring came and the prophecies of the Ghost Dance failed to materialize, the dancing would stop of its own accord. James McLaughlin, the long-time agent at the Standing Rock Reservation also saw no need for panic.

Newsmen amplified and spread the fear and panic. Over twenty correspondents were at Pine Ridge at one time or another during the four months the army occupied the reservation.[57] Many of these people were "space writers," not accredited reporters,[58] some, such as William F. Kelly, an office clerk for the *Nebraska* (Lincoln) *State Journal,* had no previous reporting experience or knowledge of Indians.[59] Because no one else could be found, Kelly was made a reporter and sent to the "seat of war." His reports are filled with embellishment, misrepresentations, and outright lies.[60] These reporters gathered in the back room of the reservation trading post and made up stories to send to their editors.[61] Their reporting of,

> Unverified rumors were presented as reports from reliable sources or eyewitness accounts, idle gossip became fact . . . a large number of the nation's newspapers indulged in a field day of exaggeration, distortion and plain faking.[62]

Even the commissioner of Indian affairs blamed the "exaggerated accounts in the newspapers" for causing the fear that brought on the flight of many Lakotas from the agencies.[63] Many young Lakotas, because of forced attendance in government schools, could read and write. In addition, many mixed bloods in the employ of the government on the reservations could also read and write. The Indians were just as frightened as the settlers by the newspaper accounts they had read. They did not want the Army to occupy their reservations and feared harm from the soldiers if they came.

Pressure on the government from panic-stricken settlers and the inexperienced agents finally brought troops to the reservations. On 18 November 1890 Major General Nelson A. Miles, commander of the Division of the Missouri, ordered Brigider General John R. Brooke, commander of the Department of the Platte, to proceed with troops from his headquarters in Omaha, Nebraska, to Pine Ridge. Miles instructed Brooke to protect the agency and to avoid hostile action if possible. Miles also advised Brooke that Royer was "alarmed and inexperienced."[64]

Brooke arrived on 19 November 1890 with a force that included the Ninth Cavalry. The Ninth was comprised of black troops led by white officers, and known as "Buffalo Soldiers" to the Indians. They were so named because their woolly hair reminded the Indians of the hair around the buffalo's head.[65]

Before the campaign was over, the following units would be present in the Dakotas: the First, Second, Seventh, Eighth, Seventeenth, and Twenty-first Infantry and the Sixth, Seventh, Eighth, and Ninth Cavalry. Units of the First and Second Artillery also served in the campaign. These troops comprised the largest consolidated force of the U.S. Army since the Civil War. In addition, units from the Nebraska National Guard stationed themselves on the southern border of the reservations to protect the citizens of Nebraska in the event of hostilities. The Federal government, at the request of the governor of South Dakota, issued arms and ammunition to private citizens who had settled along the reservations' boundaries. Colonel M. H. Day of the South Dakota Militia, under orders from Governor Mellette, distributed guns and ammunition to settlers surrounding the reservations, most notable, the Cheyenne River reservation. One newspaper account stated that over one hundred guns were distributed to civilians.[66]

Along with an army this large came the inherent problems of logistics. Not the least of these problems was the assembling of a medical department to attend wounded in need of treatment in case of hostilities. Medical personnel were brought in from all over the country. A hospital corps was assembled and, headed by Lieutenant Colonel Dallas Bache, staffed by twenty-two doctors eventually including Dr. Lauderdale, and several hospital stewards.[67]

The appearance of troops naturally alarmed the Lakota, who were already confused by the reduction of rations, the inter-tribal strife caused by the 1889 land agreement, and excitement over the Ghost Dance. Fear intensified to the point that some leaders took their people to a remote area of the Bad Lands where they thought they would be safe from attacks by the soldiers and free to dance. Many who accompanied the dancers to the Bad Lands were not followers of the new religion but fled only out of fear of the soldiers.[68]

As many as 3,500 Indians were reported in the Bad Lands.[69] They gathered on a portion of the high, inaccessible plateau called Cuny Table, they felt safe from the army. This small area became known to the army as the Stronghold. The number of Lakotas at the Stronghold reported by the army is, however, unreasonably high. After several years of drought, the Stronghold could not have physically supported the number of people claimed to be there. The native grasses had deteriorated to the point of being inadequate to support the livestock that would have been required to transport 3,500 people and their effects. The natural springs, referred to by many historians as a source of drinking water, had dried up and thus adequate water was not available for the people or their horses. Some reports claimed that the Lakotas took cattle with them to the Stronghold, but that too would not have been possible, considering the lack of grass and water. The Stronghold encompassed only 384 acres, and livestock in the numbers claimed in official reports would have required much more grazing land even under the best of climatic conditions. Therefore food for a group this size would have been an insurmountable problem, as the Lakota had no extra rations to carry with them.

General Nelson A. Miles was the overall commander of the troops. Although he initially worked from his headquarters in Chicago, Miles knew the Indians. He had many years of experience dealing with and fighting Indians. He saw action against the Sioux in the 1870s, and had been involved in campaigns against Sitting Bull, Crazy Horse, and Lame Deer. He captured Chief Joseph and his Nez Perce in 1877, and was credited with the capture of Geronimo and his Apaches in the 1880s.[70] He was sympathetic to the Lakota's problems.[71]

Miles had hopes of concluding the troubles without bloodshed. To this end, he devised a plan that included attempting to persuade as many of the ghost dancers as possible to return to their homes.[72] The army would then encircle those who remained defiant. The plan involved placing troops on three sides of the "hostiles" who remained in the Bad Lands, leaving the south end open. Miles stationed troops in a line from Oelrichs, South Dakota, northeast down the Cheyenne River to the mouth of Rapid Creek. The line then went east to the White River. This would keep the Indians on the reservation and out of the white settlements. Miles hoped the Indians would move toward the agency at Pine Ridge and surrender peacefully.[73] In mid-December Miles moved his headquarters to Rapid City, which allowed him more direct supervision of his plan.

By 18 December, some 1,500 of the "hostiles" had returned to the agency at Pine Ridge.[74] However, in some outlying camps and remote reservations the new religion was thriving. On Standing Rock and Cheyenne River reservations, the dancing continued. Bands of Miniconjou, Lakotas, under the leadership of Chiefs Hump and Big Foot, continued to dance on the Cheyenne River Reservation. Both groups had made their camp near Cherry

Creek. On the Standing Rock Reservation, Sitting Bull's Hunkpapa Lakota also continued to dance. These leaders and their followers had been classified as "hostile" by the army because of their traditionalist beliefs. They believed in the new religion and resisted the cultural changes being forced on them by the whites.

Troops in the Cheyenne River area were under the command of Colonel E. V. Sumners. Sumners was assigned the task of observing Hump, Big Foot, and their bands, and of protecting the settlers in the area. These troops had been in the area since November, and Sumners had met with Big Foot on several occasions. The two leaders developed a mutual trust and respect for each other. Through their meetings, Big Foot had convinced Sumners of his peaceful intentions.

General Miles devised a plan that would reduce the number of dancers at Cherry Creek. He knew of the friendship based on mutual trust and respect between Chief Hump and Captain Ezra P. Ewers of the Fifth Infantry, and issued orders for Ewers to report to Fort Bennett from his station in Texas. Ewers met with Hump and persuaded him and most of his followers to renounce the Ghost Dance and return to Fort Bennett. Some of Hump's followers chose to remain with Big Foot's band on Cherry Creek.[75]

After Hump's defection, Sumners received orders to bring Big Foot and his band to Fort Bennett. This action would prevent them from joining the "hostile" force still believed to be in the Bad Lands. The two leaders held talks and Big Foot consented to move his people under Sumner's escort to the fort.

Historians disagree on the role played by Sitting Bull in the Ghost Dance movement. Some claim that he was an ardent supporter and urged his people to follow the new religion. Others argue that he merely tolerated the movement. Whether or not he supported it, he believed in his people's right to dance if they so chose.[76]

On 15 December 1890, a party of Lakota policemen, under orders from the government agent James McLaughlin, killed Chief Sitting Bull while attempting to arrest him. The circumstances surrounding his death are still the subject of much debate. Regardless of the circumstances, most Lakotas believed that he was assassinated, and his death had a profound effect on all the Lakota people. His demise was due to his long-standing opposition to any further secession of lands or cooperation with the whites in any way.

After the death of Sitting Bull, many of his followers fled, in fear for their lives. On 17 December, about thirty-eight of them found their way to Big Foot's camp on Cherry Creek. Big Foot opened his camp to the refugees, where he and his followers fed and clothed them as best they could, sharing what little they had and making the refugees feel welcome.[77]

The arrival of Sitting Bull's Hunkapapas and the news of his death brought more fear and alarm to Big Foot's people. Sitting Bull was greatly respected by the Lakota. His death was the latest in a long string of assassinations of prominent Indian leaders—leaders who did not conform to what the government considered progressive. The Lakota believed that if the government would murder such a prominent man, they would not hesitate to kill again to enforce their policy of assimilation on the Lakota.

Accepting an invitation from Red Cloud, chief of the Oglala Lakota at Pine Ridge, Big Foot set off for the agency at Pine Ridge.[78] The Lakota under the leadership of Big Foot numbered approximately 370, of which 111 were "warriors." This figure includes some of Hump's band and Sitting Bull's followers. By going to Pine Ridge, Big Foot broke his word to Colonel Sumner, who was responsible for bringing Big Foot and his band to Fort Bennett. Big Foot had promised the Colonel that he would take his people to Fort Bennett.[79] Several things factored into his decision to go to Pine Ridge, however, perhaps the most compelling of which was the message Big Foot received from a settler named John Dunn, who was sent by Colonel Sumners to talk to Big Foot. Dunn's mission was to find out when Big Foot intended to take his people to Fort Bennett. Dunn told Big Foot that if he stayed on the Cheyenne River, the soldiers would open fire on the village during the night. According to Dunn, the only way for Big Foot to avoid a fight with Sumner was to flee to Pine Ridge.[80]

The army speculated that Big Foot was on his way to join the other "hostiles" assumed to be in the Bad Lands. As illustrated by the map (see fig. 4), Big Foot was not going toward the Stronghold in the Bad Lands but to the agency at Pine Ridge. Units were ordered to the field to locate and obtain the surrender of Big Foot and his followers. On 28 December 1890 elements of the Seventh Cavalry and First Artilery under the command of Major Sammuel M. Whitside intercepted this cold, tired, hungry band of Lakota on the main road near Porcupine Butte en route to the agency at Pine Ridge. Big Foot, ill with pneumonia and not wanting a fight, promptly surrendered to

Troop I of the Seventh U.S. Cavalry at Pine Ridge 1890. Photograph by Clarence G. Morledge, courtesy of Rohan Collection, Nebraska State Historical Society.

Whitside. Had Big Foot's intentions been hostile, he most likely would have fought there, as he held the high ground and his women and children were well behind the lines.[81] Without further incident, the Lakota and their captors moved to Wounded Knee Creek to camp for the night.

During the night, Whitside was reinforced by the remainder of the Seventh Cavalry led by Colonel James Forsyth, who assumed command of the entire force. The army units included the Seventh Cavalry and Light Battery E of the First Artillery. The artillery unit came equipped with two additional rapid-fire Hotchkiss mountain cannons. Total command strength was in excess of 487 troops and four Hotchkiss guns.[82] There was also one company of Indian Scouts under the command of Captain C. W. Taylor.

Forsyth's orders were to disarm the Lakota and take them to the railhead at Gordon, Nebraska, where they would be transported south and held until the troubles passed. The Lakota men were assembled in a council ring on the morning of 29 December and ordered by Colonel Forsyth to surrender their arms. The council was held in front of the tent used to house the ailing Chief Big Foot.[83] Troops had been stationed facing each other in a hollow square surrounding the Lakota. (see fig. 5)[84] Some of the Lakota returned to their

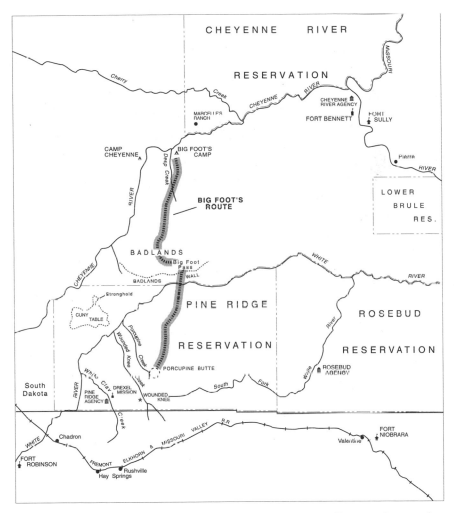

Figure 4. Big foot's Route from the Cheyenne River Reservation to the Agency at Pine Ridge

The wagon full of Lakota women and children fired upon by the Hotchkiss guns of Captain Capron's Artillery. Photo courtesy of the Nebraska State Historical Society.

camp and brought their guns back to the soldiers. Fearing that some weapons were still concealed, Forsyth ordered a physical search of the Lakota men present in the council, along with a search of the camp.

The search of the camp caused confusion, excitement and fear among the women and children.[85] During the confusion, a shot was fired. No one can say with certainty which side fired the first shot, and the question may never be satisfactorily answered. At the sound of that first shot, however, the troops opened fire.

The number of armed Lakota at that moment is another much-disputed point. Most historians agree at least some of the Lakota men had concealed rifles under their blankets, but the vast majority were unarmed. Colonel Forsyth reported taking forty-eight guns prior to the fight.[86] Captain Charles B. Ewing, a military surgeon at the site, puts the number of armed warriors at forty-two.[87]

Reports on Lakota casualties differ. Experts disagree on the number of killed and wounded, with some authorities putting the total numbers killed at 260.[88] It is known that many of the wounded Lakota suffered from multiple gunshot wounds, several had compound fractures, and a few had multiple compound fractures. Some had both multiple gunshot wounds and compound fractures.[89] It would be safe to assume as well that many of those killed also suffered from multiple wounds.

It is clear that once the fighting started, the officers lost control of the young inexperienced troopers. They inflicted casualties on their own troops in a cross-fire, and the officers were unable, or unwilling, to stop their men from firing indiscriminately, and carnage ensued.[90]

Many women and children fell prey to the soldiers' bullets and fire from the cannon. A wagon loaded with women and children was fired on by the Hotchkiss cannon, killing or wounding all on board.[91] Most of the women and children were killed in the ravine behind the Lakota camp where they had fled to seek refuge.

Of the soldiers killed, many suffered multiple wounds. It was reported that Captain George D. Wallace, the commanding officer of Company K, suffered multiple wounds. The large number of casualties in Companies A, B, I, and K supports the conclusion that a great many casualties were the result of crossfire.[92]

In a confidential letter, Miles said of the fight,

Wholesale massacre occurred and I have never heard of a more brutal, cold blooded massacre than that at Wounded Knee. About two hundred women and children were killed and wounded; women with little children on their backs, and small children powder-burned by the men who killed them being so near as to burn the flesh and clothing with the powder of their guns, and nursing babes with five bullet holes through them. . . . Col. Forsyth is responsible for allowing the command to remain where it was stationed after he assumed command, and in allowing his troops to be in such a position that the line of fire of every troop was in direct line of their own comrades, or their camp.[93]

Medical reports of multiple high-caliber gunshot wounds to the soldiers support the allegations of crossfire due to the poor placement of the troops.

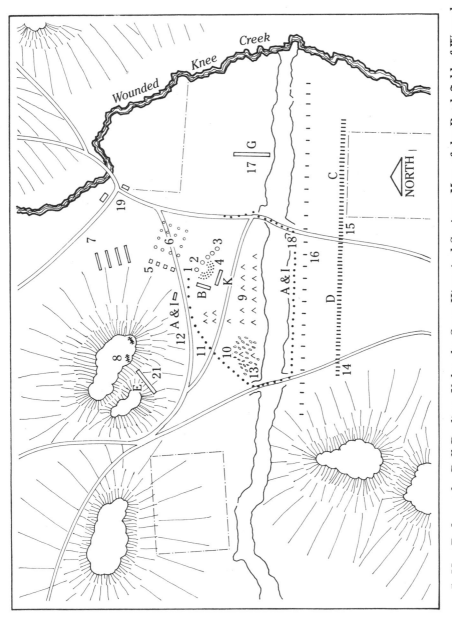

Figure 5. Map Redrawn by Dell Darling, Nebraska State Historical Society. Map of the Battlefield of Wounded Knee Creek. (From a map in the James W. Forsyth papers, Beinecke Library, Yale University.)

Key to fig. 5

"A&I" = 76 men from A&I troops forming dismounted line of sentinels.

"A&I" = Detachments from A&I troops.

"B" = Troop B dismounted in line.

"C" = Troop C mounted in line (Sorrel troop).

"D" = Troop D mounted in line (Black troop).

"E" = Troop E mounted in line (Bay troop).

"G" = Troop G mounted in line (Gray troop).

"K" = Troop K dismounted in line.

1. = Scout tent from which hostile buck shot two soldiers.

2. = Tent occupied by Big Foot and his wife in front of which Big Foot was killed.

3. = Tents put up for the use of the hostiles.

4. = Council ring in or around which were Major Whitside, Captain. Varnum, Captain. Hoff, Lieutenant Robinson, Lieutenant Nichelson, Dr. Glennan, Captain Wallace; and near which were General. Forsyth, Lieutenant. McCormick, and some reporters.

5. = Officers' tents, Seventh Battalion.

6. = Enlisted men's tents, Seventh Battalion.

7. = Bivouac of the Second Battalion on the night of 28 December 1890.

8. = Four Hotchkiss guns and detachment of the First Artillery under Captain Capron, and Second Lieutenant. Hawthorne Second Artillery.

9. = Indian village.

10. = Indian ponies.

11. = Dismounted line of sentinels.

12. = Captains Ilsely and Moylan.

13. = Lieutenants Garlington and Waterman.

14. = Captains Godfrey and Second Lieutenant Tompkins.

15. = Captain Jackson and Lieutenant Donaldson.

16. = Lieutenant Taylor, Ninth Cavalry, commanding Indian scouts.

17. = Captain Edgerly and Lieutenant Brewer.

18. = Captain Nowlan and Lieutenant Gresham.

19. = Shacks.

20. = Bend of ravine in which a number of hostiles took refuge and from which Lieutenant Hawthorne was shot.

21. = Lieutenants Sickel and Rice.

Note: The "medicine men" was hideously painted in blue, green, and yellow. All the bucks while in the council ring had on blankets with their guns, principally Winchesters, concealed under them. Most of the bucks were painted and wore "Ghost Shirts." Captain Wallace was found near the center of the council ring. Big Foot was killed two-three yards in front of his tent. Father Craft was near center of ring when stabbed. Indians broke to the west through B and K Troops.

**Wounded Lakota prisoners inside the Episcopal Church at Pine Ridge.
Photograph courtesy of the South Dakota State Historical Society.**

Officers who were present provide further evidence.[94] Dr. Ewing stated, "I have reason to believe that some of our men were killed by the fire of others of our troops. I base it from the position of the troops. Most injury was inflicted upon Captain Wallace's Troop K . . . Located as the troops were, and firing as they did, it was impossible not to wound or kill each other."[95]

News of the massacre soon spread to the bands who had started to return to Pine Ridge. Fear and panic swept through the villages. They fled either toward the Bad Lands or moved to White Clay Creek, farther away from the troops. On hearing the news of Wounded Knee, the Lakota who were returning to the agency to surrender turned back. (Miles put this number at 4,000 which is questionable.[96])

Small groups of young men sought revenge and staged attacks on remote parts of the reservation. A force of Lakota under Chief Two Strikes rode to Wounded Knee Creek and attacked the troops who had just massacred their kinsmen. Another group of Brule from Two Strikes' band opened fire on the agency that same day. The Lakota went from the verge of surrender to open hostility in a matter of hours.[97]

Fear and confusion consumed both sides. Friendly Lakota now feared retaliation by the soldiers. The hostile Lakota wanted to avenge their dead kinsmen. The soldiers, most without experience in Indian country, feared an attack on their positions. Breastworks and other fortifications were ordered erected. No one could predict what would happen next.

The troops with their dead and wounded, along with many wounded Lakota, returned to the agency later the same day. The wounded soldiers were quartered in the field hospital. Most of the wounded Lakota were housed in the Episcopal church, which was modified to serve as a hospital. The pews were removed and straw was scattered on the floor for the wounded to lie on. Agent Royer reported fifty-one wounded Lakota at the agency: four men and forty-seven women and children. Dr. Ives' records indicate for only thirty-five Lakota received treatment for wounds.[98]

The next day, 30 December, a group of Indians staged an attack on a supply train within two miles of the agency. The Ninth Cavalry, under the command of Colonel Guy V. Henry, had ridden fifty miles that day to the Bad Lands to scout the area near the Stronghold and look for signs of the Lakota. The Buffalo Soldiers were successful in driving off the wagon train's attackers. These Lakota then proceeded to the Drexel Mission near White Clay Creek. Colonel Henry returned with his men to the agency, having ridden over one hundred miles in the preceding 24 hours.

Later that morning General Brooke ordered Forsyth to the Catholic Mission, where hostile Lakotas had been reportedly seen. He led his eight companies of cavalry and a unit of artillery with two Hotchkiss guns to the mission. Forsyth found the mission had not been attacked, but some abandoned outbuildings had been set on fire.[99] He was ready to return to his camp when one of his scouts reported shots fired from the general direction of a known Lakota encampment on White Clay Creek. Forsyth marched his entire force or more than four hundred men plus artillery in the direction of the gunfire through a valley, ignoring the strategic value of the high ground. The Indians soon occupied the high ground and had Forsyth pinned down on three sides. The force that surrounded Forsyth consisted of sixty to seventy teenage Indian boys, most of whom did not have rifles but carried only clubs.[100] The shooting Forsyth's scouts had heard was Lakotas camped along the White Clay Creek killing beef. A request for assistance was sent to General Brooke.[101] The timely arrival of Colonel Henry and his Buffalo Soldiers of the Ninth Cavalry saved Forsyth and his troops from a disaster much like the one at Little Big Horn.

Losses from this encounter included one officer, Lieutenant Mann, and one wounded enlisted man, who was left behind to be found by the Indians. This soldier, Private Chetti, was scalped to avenge the mutilations of victims at Wounded Knee, some of whom had been scalped.[102]

These were some of the events Lauderdale was reading about during his journey from the east. The day of Lauderdale's arrival saw more fighting and uncertainty, which would continue for several more days.

On 3 January a detachment of the Sixth Cavalry was attacked several miles to the north of the agency, and on 5 January there was further action near Wounded Knee Creek. On 7 January Lieutenant E. W. Casey of the Twenty Second Infantry was killed. In command of a troop of Cheyenne Scouts camped near White Clay Creek, Casey went out to observe a hostile camp of Brules. He rode a short distance from the camp and, while talking to some Lakota, was shot by a young Brule warrior named Plenty Horses, who had just ridden up.[103] Many thought it was an act of cold-blooded murder. Plenty Horses had recently returned from the Carlisle Indian School in Pennsylvania and some of his peers looked upon him with disdain, calling him white. The whites would not accept him either, because although he was educated, he was still an Indian. To prove himself to his people, he shot Lieutenant Casey. Such attacks became more isolated and hostilities were winding down. Surrender of the remaining hostiles seemed imminent.

On 31 December 1890 General Miles moved his headquarters from Rapid City to Pine Ridge, where he assumed direct control of the situation. On 4 January General Miles relieved Colonel Forsyth of command, charging him with disobedience and incompetence for putting his men in positions that caused casualties from their own crossfire and causing the deaths of numerous noncombatants at Wounded Knee.[104] Forsyth's actions at the Drexel Mission fight helped convince Miles of the colonel's ineffectiveness as a field commander.

Miles appointed a board of inquiry to investigate the charges against Forsyth. The board consisted of three officers, Colonel Eugene A. Carr, Major J. Ford Kent, and Captain Frank D. Baldwin. Colonel Carr, however, resigned from the board because of the political pressures he knew would come to bear on the members.[105] Desiring a quick end to the sordid affair, pressure did indeed come from Washington, thus making the board's job nearly impossible. The investigation, perhaps yielding to this pressure,[106] concluded that Colonel Forsyth was not culpable. Captain Baldwin did believe a massacre had taken place, but for reasons known only to him his report helped to exonerate Forsyth.[107] In a letter to G. W. Baird General Miles said,

> I do not think there has ever been as marked an illustration of the suppression of the truth and false impressions published broadcast as there was in the affairs of last winter. . . not an exoneration of Forsyth, but a personal assault upon myself.[108]

In the aftermath of the Kent-Baldwin investigation, it is theorized that the officers of the Seventh Cavalry saw a need to persuade the general public that the Wounded Knee "affair" was indeed a battle and not a massacre. Such a campaign would take pressure off the high command in Washington and counteract much of the unfavorable attention the army was receiving in the press. One tactic was to fabricate heroes. To accomplish this, many of the soldiers involved were recommended for brevet promotions, certificates of merit, mention in orders, and the Congressional Medal of Honor. In all, thirty two men were named for their actions in the Wounded Knee fight, not including those officers recommended for brevet promotion. A total of twenty-five men were recommended for the Congressional Medal of Honor, and of these twenty were awarded.[109]

The Seventh Cavalry never showed regret for their actions at Wounded Knee. As time passed, they went so far as to become boastful. For example in the history of their regiment, one of their officers later wrote,

> The prompt and drastic punishment awarded treachery at Wounded Knee contributed in no small measure towards bringing the hostile Indians to a realizing sense of their obligation to comply with the demands of the government.[110]

On 11 January a small party of peaceful Oglala Lakotas from Pine Ridge were attacked while returning from a hunt in the Black Hills, by a group of local cowboys. The party consisted of two families: Few Tails, a peaceful old

A group of Seventh Cavalry Officers at Pine Ridge 1891. (1) H. G. Sickel, (2) Unknown, (3) Miles Moylan, (4) Lloyd S. McCormick, (5) John C. Gresham, (6) S. M. Whitside, (7) William J. Nicholson, (8) Ezra B. Fuller, (9) J. E. Maxfield, (10) Civilian not known. Photograph courtesy of the Nebraska State Historical Society.

man, and his wife, along with One Feather, his wife and two children. The hunt was authorized and the party had obtained the required pass from Royer, granting permission to leave the bounds of the reservation. Their pass was in fact checked by soldiers the night prior to the attack at their campsite at the mouth of Alkali Creek.[111] When they resumed their journey the next morning, they had gone only about 300 yards when they were ambushed by a party of white men hiding near the road. The first shots killed Few Tails and two of the ponies that were hitched to his wagon. His wife received two bullet wounds, but was not killed. One Feather's wife was also wounded. The whites pursued One Feather and his family for about 18 miles before giving up, and the Lakota eventually reached the safety of the agency.[112]

Few Tails' wife remained unconscious until the next morning, when she awoke to find her husband dead. Locating one of their extra ponies, she rode all day until she reached a settler's house. Instead of finding help, she was threatened at gunpoint. She fled in such a hurry that she left her horse. She traveled on foot only at night because of her fear of the whites. Weak from her two bullet wounds, one in her breast and one in the leg, it took her five days for her to reach the beef corral near the agency, where she was found by some soldiers and taken to safety and medical attention.[113]

With the hostilities over, the Ghost Dancers and those who had joined with them out of fear of the army slowly filtered back to the agency at Pine Ridge. The ring of troops slowly tightened around them, forcing their return. By 12 January these Lakota were in sight of the agency, and on 15 January 1891 General Miles accepted their formal surrender.[114]

The last Indian war was over. The surrender was unconditional and the Lakota even surrendered their arms, something that rarely happened. In the end almost six hundred firearms were turned over to the army.[115] Miles also demanded the surrender of the leaders of the Ghost Dance movement. Kicking Bear, Short Bull, and twenty-three others were taken prisoner.[116] Miles did agree to send a delegation of Lakotas to Washington to discuss their grievances with the appropriate officials,[117] and he also agreed to have army officers serve as Indian agents. This was something he had wanted all along, but he let the Lakotas believe that he was making concessions.

Later in January, General Miles held a grand review of all the troops. The review was planned as more of a show of strength to impress the Indians than anything else. Shortly after the review, the units started dispersing, returning to their original posts. This process would take several weeks. On 26 January Miles left for Chicago with twenty-five Indian prisoners, all former leaders of the Ghost Dance,[118] being held to ensure that peace was kept.

General Miles also figured in an interesting footnote to the ambush of Few Tails and the killing of Lieutenant Casey: The civil authorities wanted Plenty Horses put on trial in Rapid City for Casey's murder, but the army was holding him at Fort Meade, and Miles refused to release him to the Justice Department until "prompt and energetic action will be taken to discover and arrest the murderers who attacked, killing one and wounding others of a party of six Indian men and two squaws while returning to Pine Ridge from a hunt . . . "[119] The controversy eventually found its way to Washington, ultimately involving the secretary of war and the attorney general.

Plenty Horses stood trial on 23 April 1891 in the Federal District Court in Sioux Falls. The trial lasted a week, and on 30 April the jury reported that it was hopelessly deadlocked. A second trial opened on 23 May, with the defense contending that a state of war existed between the Lakota Nation and the U.S. Army. The district attorney wanted General Miles to testify that there had been no war, but Miles refused. Had he not refused to testify and admitted at the trial that a state of war did not exist, those involved in the massacre at Wounded Knee Creek could have been tried for murder. The judge at the second trial was convinced by the defense's arguments and ordered the jury to acquit Plenty Horses.

The cowboys who killed Few Tails went to trial in Sturgis, South Dakota. On 2 July 1891 they were found not guilty by a jury of their peers.[120] The acquittal reflects the attitude held toward the Lakota by the settlers in the area, one of the contributing factors to the situation that led to the tragedy at Wounded Knee.

Chapter Two

The Letters

Dear Joe,

Reached Syracuse and found Central Train 40 minutes late. Took sleeper for Chicago. Felt tired and sleepy, went to my berth early. Slept some, but would have preferred my little bed at Ft O[ntario]. Reached Detroit at 8 A.M. Good breakfast feel better for it. Papers contain more particulars of the fight near the Agency at Pine Ridge.[1] There must be a great need of Medical Officers to look after the wounded and my services are needed more [there] than at Ft. O[ntario] in my special lines. I hope this will be a comfort to you during my absence.

The snow is fast disappearing, and there is where we are this moment only a little to be seen. I hope you are not going to lose your snow and those nice rides in the new sleigh when it comes. It is raining some and looks far from pleasant.

Shall reach Chicago about $4^{1}/_{2}$ [4:30] P.M. where I shall mail this. I shall go this evening to Omaha reaching there Friday morning, the 2nd inst. Will then call at Hd Qtrs and ascertain how to pursue my route further.

A gentleman, Rev. Chas. Gardner is a passenger with me enroute to Omaha, and says many of the Army people, Gen'l Brooke and others are members of his flock. Mr. G[ardner] used to visit Oswego and remembers when [he was] a boy, going to see Ft. Ontario.

43

Marshall[2]
12 P.M.

Station for dinner. Do not have any appetite so stopped to get a sand-
wich and fried cakes for my satchel and eat it when I feel like it. A driz-
zling rain all the time, no snow, and they say more this side of Chicago.

I hope Julia[3] will come on soon so that you will have company. Mr.
Gardner says he must hurry home to Omaha to comfort the wives of
Officers left behind there [by those] who have gone to the front. Some
of whom are of his congregation. $1^1/_2$ [1:30] P.M.. No rain just now 07
miles from Chicago.

Niles Mich.

A band of music at the station to greet us.
I shall not be able to give you any information of the Sioux War till I
get farther West.

With a heart full of love to you and the children, I remain

J.V.L.

4 P.M. Just entered Chicago all OK.

J.

No. Fork of Elkhorn, Neb.
Fri. Jan. 2, 1891, 2 p.m.

Dear Joe,

The train is waiting 25 min. for dinner. I have been taking a cup of
coffee as I had a good breakfast and do not care to take too much food,
as my appetite is never very good on the cars.

Have been riding thro a fine corn and grass region with small villages here and there. No forests but the lines of poplars that sit in rows
to break the wind. A beautiful sun shining day. It does not seem that
you should be buried in snow as I left you.

Wednesday eve

There are two young ladies on the sleeper, several gentlemen, and we have discussed the Indian War, we have reached the conclusion that the Ghost Dance has nothing to do with the cause, but that the Indian Bureau from Commissioner Morgan[4] down are a bad lot and that the Indians have been starved into making their depredations. That this is the real cause of their discontent.

We reach Rushville about 2 in the morning [where we will] proceed north to the Agency at Pine Ridge. Have telegraphed for transportation and an escort to meet us.

We have endorsed the cartoon on the first page of the . . . newspaper . . . for Jan. 3, 1891, which you must get and see if you do not agree with us. The Indian has the tent poles but nothing to cover them with and so has to "dance" to keep warm.

Rushville, Nebraska, 1890, the railhead for troops and supplies moving to Pine Ridge. Photograph courtesy of the Nebraska State Historical Society.

Saturday Morning
Rushville

Reached here last night about 2 o'clock had the company of Bishop Hare,[5] whom you know. He goes to Pine Ridge to look after his church and schools that are located there. There has been no fighting since

Tuesday. We will all leave this morning for the Agency, Capt. Ruhlen AQM[6] is here at Rushville and has charge of the transportation to and from this point to the Agency.

Rushville is a town of 400 or 500 consisting of [stone] residences, and like any other Railroad town.

Weather keen and cold but little snow. I can not tell you any thing of affairs at the Agency till I reach there myself.

A bright and beautiful day and I wish that this Indian trouble was at an end and we were on our way home.

With a great deal of love to you and the children I remain,

Yours Lovingly,

J.V. Lauderdale

One of the stagecoaches that served as public conveyances between Rushville, Nebraska, and the Agency at Pine Ridge. Photograph by Clarence G. Morledge, courtesy of Rohan Collection Nebraska State Historical Society.

Pine Ridge Agency, S.D.
Jan. 3, 1891

Dear Joe,

This morning Bishop Hare rose before me, and made his way to the breakfast room of the Commercial House at an early hour. We looked up the Q.M. here at Rushville, and made our request for transportation to this Agency. We were not sure if the road here was open, so we telegraphed to Capt. Humphries [Humphrey][7] but the stage coach started before us, and as there were other teams starting to go out we decided not to wait for an answer.

About 9 a.m. we three Doctors piled into an open Jersy bench wagon with three seats, and taking our satchels and making ourselves comfortable with felt boots, and my buffalo robe, and such other wraps as the livery man provided we set out. Our road took us over a country much like the lands between Puma and . . . Many acres are wire fenced and have yielded splendid crops of wheat and corn, I should judge by the stubble. These grounds are sprinkled with light snow and people never think of sleigh riding as they are not favored with enough snow. The sky was beautifully clear and the sun though not warm was more genial than you are favored with.

Bishop Hare, and a Jesuit Priest came in a carriage by themselves some times going before, sometimes behind us. I had in the seat with me Dr. McGillycuddy, a very intelligent ex-physician and who for five or six years had been Indian Agent at this place, as my companion.[8]

I will not try to add any more to this as everything is confusion. They are sending all the wounded who are able to Ft. Riley.

I saw Capt. Moylan[9] and he wished to be remembered to you. Capt. M[oylan] lost some men,[10] but was not scratched himself.

With love to you and the children, I remain,

Your loving husband,
J.V. Lauderdale

P.S. W[eather] is cool and delightful.

Pine Ridge Agency S.D.
Sunday Noon Jan. 4, 1891

Dear Joe,

When we approached this Post yesterday we found over 300 Tepees near the Post occupied with friendly Indians and their families. At a little distance off we could see a group of Indian women and hear the beating of the Tom-Tom, the music they were dancing around to. You would be surprised to see what a great multitude of friendlies there are in and around this post.

Capt. Humphries [Humphrey] the Q.M. loaned me some blankets, and Lt. Mallory[11] comsry [commissary officer] of Gen'l Brooke[12] gave me a place in his snug Sibley. So that I had a very comfortable bed last night. Have not had such a good rest since I left home. I reported to Gen'l Miles,[13] and found him with a smooth shaven face and did not recognize him from his photos we have seen at the Baldwins.[14] Did I tell you Capt. B[aldwin] is here? He came in yesterday and is on some kind of staff duty. Have not seen him yet.

Six ambulances and a few other wagons left here for Rushville removing the wounded, or as many as could travel. They will be sent to Ft. Riley for treatment. Lt. Garlinghouse [Garlington][15] was of the number. The women and children are cared for by our Doctors and it is a strange sight in more ways than one. All the wounded Soldiers are in Sibley tents and so are many of the Indians. Many of the Indians are in the Episcopal Church. Bishop Hare [and] Rev. Mr. Cook[16] invited me to the service tent. There was so much going on that interested me that I could not see my duty in that direction, at least not this morning.

A peace conference is going on today, the results have not transpired we all hope matters can be settled without more fighting. There are many reports in the papers that you need not believe. There are half a dozen reporters in the room where I am waiting for lunch who are writing for their bread and spin long yarns for their readers. They are a very ordinary set of fellows and their opinions are of little value.[17]

Capt. Capron[18] was in our tent last evening telling how he worked his light battery on the Indians in the last fight. He made destructive work with the enemy and seemed to take delight in it.

Captain Allyn Capron, First U.S. Artillery. Photograph courtesy of the United States Army Military History Institute.

I met Lt. Fuller[19] of the 7th Cavalry and he is busy . . . Gray hair sprinkled his beard with white.

Such beautiful weather you have seen only in a Texas winter. It is about as cold as we had it in Texas at the coldest time last winter.

Dr. Evart [Ewing][20] one of our party has been assigned duty with a battalion of the 7th Cavalry.

Some of Capron's artillery at Pine Ridge, 1891. (Note these are not Hotchkiss guns like those used against the Lakota at Wounded Knee.) Photograph courtesy of the Nebraska State Historical Society.

Interior of the Episcopal church that served as a hospital for the wounded Lakota prisoners at Pine Ridge. Photograph by Clarence G. Morledge, courtesy of Rohan Collection, Nebraska State Historical Society.

Sunday Evening

Was over to the Episcopal Church and assisted Dr. Ives[21] (brother of
the Lt. 10th Infty) in dressing a little Indian babe who was shot thro
the back of it's thigh.[22] There were at least twenty other cases of gunshot wounds in men, women, and children living in the nave and alcove
of the little church. It carries one back to war time to see a church
turned into a hospital.

Dr. Eastman[23] the Indian Agency physician is a full blooded Dakota
and graduated at Dartmouth Coll. and appears like an intelligent prac-
titioner. Bishop Hare likes him very much.

Capt. Baldwin went out to the grounds where the battle was fought
not the battle, but the treacherous attack on the troops when they
attempted to disarm the Indians. And hereby will hang a tale that will
be investigated in due time, and I fear that the Officer who did not use
precautionary measures to prevent the treacherous assault will be
brought to give an account of himself. You recall the occurrence –the
most disastrous affair of the whole campaign. 84 bucks and 64 women
and children were killed at the above affair, so says the latest
account.[24]

Rested better last evening than the first night as the place was
rather new to me, and I had not gotten used to my environment.

Was in Capt. Baldwin's tent and he looks fat and ruddy and wished
to be remembered to you. He is having a good time, and this kind of
place just suits him. He says Netu B[aldwin] is in New York. I told him
to tell her to send her card to Kad and I thought the latter would call
upon her. I was very glad to see Baldwin. I hear nothing new as to the
condition of things. There are a good many things to write about, but I
must send these scraps now.

With lots of love to you and the children, I remain,

Your loving husband,
J.V. Lauderdale

Captain and Assistant Surgeon Robert J. Gibson. Photograph courtesy of the Prints and Photographs Collection, History of Medicine Division, National Library of Medicine, Bethesda, Maryland.

Pine Ridge Agency S.D.
Mon. Jan. 5th, 1891

Dear Joe,

I am seated in my tent (Lt. Mallory's) after lunch, and while I rest I will begin scribbling a little to you. It's a beautiful day just like a winter at Ft. Davis. Have been here three days, and have nothing of duty assigned me. Went through Dr. Erven's [Ewing's] hospital and he showed me half a dozen cases of pretty gunshot wounds. No ghastly cases, no men in racking pain, although one poor fellow had a pistol ball wound traversing his face from cheek to cheek.[25] All doing as well as could be expected. I walked over to the Episcopal Church and looked over some of the cases of the Indians. Dr. Gibson[26] (who is all the way from Ft Trumball came to attend this circus) conducted me through. The Indians have plenty of hay for their beds and this with their blankets give them as good accommodations as they require.

Miss Elaine Goodale[27] a good missionary, tending to the wants of these unfortunates by giving them broths and soups, Miss G[oodale] has been with the Sioux for four years and speaks the language to some extent. Before I had completed my walk among the wounded Miss G. asked me to visit a Sioux that had for some time been her escort among the schools. He was living in a neighboring cottage. Taking an interpreter with me, I walked over to the house and found a stout young man. He had been caring for the sick in the Chapel, and all the labor and sickening sights were too much for his nerves and he yielded. An old depressed fracture of the skull (the more remote cause) I discovered by inquiring of the wife who sat by the bed ministering to his wants. Writing some simple prescription I left the young man and made the case more fully known to Miss. G[oodale].

Our side of the hospital we have but about 8 patients. This number divided among twelve, or fourteen surgeons does not give much professional business. Dr. Bache[28] has not assigned me to anything yet. He telegraphed to Greenleaf[29] "What should he do with us?" I would go home tomorrow if I could.

Reports come in that Red Cloud, one of the hostile chiefs, is on his way here. Mr. Cook, the missionary says he will believe it when it happens.

Red Cloud's House. Photograph by Clarence G. Morledge, courtesy of James Flavin.

Four o'clock

Guard mounting, some of the troops have this with drum and fife while others call the men together with the bugle.

Capt Baldwin says Mrs. B[aldwin] is at Davis yet, but they are all packed up ready for a start. He has been on a practice march this winter, and Dr. Skinner[30] was along as Medical Officer.

The wind blows up fresh and cool this evening and we get some dust in our Sibley tent.

The First Infty. from California under command of Col. Shafter[31] are here and I have just been assigned to duty with that regiment. They are now stationed here as a home guard, and have their tents pitched at two or three places on the ridges half a mile from the Post, and one company with Hd. Qtrs. Band just in front of the Episcopal Church. I will enclose a print showing the Church and the tents. I have another photo print showing the Agency Buildings which I will send also and you can form some idea of the place.

Everybody wishes the question of fighting, or no fighting could be settled and we could go to our respective posts.

You may just keep these photo prints carefully as they are the best I can get and will be interesting to refer to.

I hope to get a line from you in a day or two as I have not had any thing since leaving home.

With a great deal of love to you and the children, I remain,

Your loving husband,

J.V. Lauderdale

First Infantry Camp, Pine Ridge, South Dakota, 1891. (Note Episcopal church on far right.) Photograph courtesy Nebraska State Historical Society.

Pine Ridge Agency S.D.

Tues. Jan. 6, 1891

Dear Joe,

I have just been taking a stroll around the agency buildings. This time I visited the large double building at the west end of the line which is used for school purposes, and find lines of sentinels patrolling up and down the outer line of defenses which have been thrown up, and which may be used if the hostiles should presume to make a raid.[32]

**The Indian Boarding School at Pine Ridge. Photograph taken by Clarence
G. Morledge, courtesy of James Flavin.**

The school is in session all the same, and the Indian girls are pouring over their books as I glance into the windows. I do not care to enter
as my mind does not descend to such peaceful pursuits as these scholars are interested.

Another Indian council is being held fifteen miles from here, and I
learn that the Indians will all come in if the present agent is removed,[33]
and an Army officer is left here to see that there is fair play for their
side.

Now don't you put any confidence in the reports about impending
battles as they exist only in the fertile brains of the reporters who have
to "grind out" news for their respective papers. And when they get an
item, they work it over and over, and add to it and connect it with
some old bit of news and thus present old things in a new dress and if
one is not mindful he imagines there is new news of more depravation.

Did I tell you that Emil Appel is here doing duty as a Hospital
Steward? Says that he and his brother could not make it pay making
ice in Sebring. That the elder Appel has gone back to Illinois to get
something to do. How their cherished hopes for making a fortune have

been dashed to the ground have melted away like a cake of ice in a Texas sun, to use another figure. And with it some of their conceit.

After supper I started out to find something of interest. Went down to Capt. Baldwin's tent but, found him closeted with Gen'l Miles and so wandered back to the Chapel. No light in Mr. Cook's parlor, returned to my tent. The camp is not lighted except as a thin white light comes through the canvas from the lamps within and it's rather unsafe walking about at night.

Later; I sally forth and find a light in Mr. C[ook]'s parlor and called. Miss Goodale and Dr. Eastman were seated in the parlor. Mrs. C[ook] is a lovely little woman and is well calculated for a missionary's wife.

Bishop Hare left yesterday and will bear to the people of the East the situation of affairs here.

After leaving Mrs. C[ook] I returned to my tent. Lt. Mallory asked me if I had met Mrs. Tibbals [Tibbles], [34] the educated Ponca, who is here with her husband. He is a reporter for an Omaha paper. I had not met the lady, and accepted an invitation to call with him and see her. Found her and husband near the Post. Mrs. T[ibbles] has French blood, as well as Indian and has been educated at Wellesley College. Her English education is far above average and she would grace any community. She told me of the wrongs that have been practiced upon the Indians, and the well-laid plans of the politicians and Indian Ring to deprive these poor people of their just dues. That when crops would fail they would often cut down on the supplies instead of making good their losses. Mrs. T[ibbles] speaking the language perfectly knows she can set the subject to true light. "Bright Eyes" is her Indian name.

Wednesday Jan. 7

It is expected Red Cloud will certainly be in today.

After breakfast Dr. Gardner (Dr. Hanes' uncle)[35] took his pipe and as he smoked, told me of his experiences at Ft. Davis, and we exchanged notes on the society of that region where we had each served. Dr. G[ardner] had a row with old Col. Breckatt[36] before he could make him keep the tadpoles and frogs out of the water tanks. He told of the Gages and the Finks, . . . among the wounded Indian prisoners in the Chapel and saw Dr. Kilborne[37] and Ives dressing the gunshot wounds. They are going to send some of the least injured to rooms in the large school building.

We thought there would be snow this morning, but it has cleared again and I find my cardigan jacket comfortable without my overcoat. Have many times wished for a detective camera to take "correct views" of things here. It is about time to mail this and I will close with love to you and the children.

Your loving husband,
J.V. Lauderdale

Pine Ridge Agency S.D.
Wed. Jan 7, 1891

Dear Joe,

Your good letter of Fri. Jan. 2 came today, the first word from you since I left home. I think I have sent some notes every day. I only regret that Julia, or someone was not there to keep you company when I left home. But the order came suddenly and I did not have time to make all my preparations complete.

I mentioned to the Q.M. of the 1st Infty with whom I messed, that Mrs. Ellis had a ten pound baby. He replied with a promptness, that he thought it would be a twenty pounder from her looks. The 1st Infty you know are from Angel Island, California.

I am glad that Vance is pleased with cow's milk, and hope you will see the milk lady from time to time, that she has good feed for her cows and then the milk will be good. I hope Julia has come on to be the company for you and the children. I have sent some items of news every day since I left you and from these disconnected notes you may be able to form some idea of the situation of affairs here.

We have just heard that Agent Royer has been removed and that an Army Officer is to be placed in charge of the agency. Thank the Lord for this move. Red Cloud the head chief of the Ogallalas [Oglala] (Sioux) is surely coming in tomorrow. One sad item of news is current viz that Lt. Casey in charge of a Company of Scouts was killed.[38] The circumstances of the affair have not been published in full.

Thursday Morning Jan. 8th

Col. Shafter CO. [Commanding Officer] of the 1st [Infantry] came yesterday with two companies of his regiment and they are setting up their tents with the others, who have been here for the past week. The paymaster is here paying the troops. Reports come this morning from the hostile camp that they have had a riff among the bucks [who] want to fight, and the remainder wish to sue for peace and refuse to let the latter come in. So there may be another hitch in the settlement of the affair.

There has always been a war between the Dept. of Interior and the War Dept. relative to the management and control of the Indians and it seems that there will be a renewal of the strife at this juncture.[39]

The Army will be a menace to any great battle on either side, and I hope they may not take any other position in this question. The total removal of all the Indian Agents of warlike Indians and placing them under the charge of Officers of the Army, who will deal with them honestly, and enable the Indian to get the full benefit of the money appropriated for them. We succeeded in disposing of the Post Trader in the Army. Now we should get rid of the Indian Post Trader who at present with his colleagues in the Indian Ring, politicians and all deprive the Indian of what is just due and reap a rich profit.

It is man's inhumanity to the Indians, that curses countless thousands tomorrow. If there was a proper administration there would be no trouble then. The Post Trader[s] are not the only ones to make trouble. The squaw men do all they can to ferment trouble among the Indians, because they can make a few dollars out of it. But it is a long subject and the mail will soon close and I will say good bye today.

Your loving husband,
J.V. Lauderdale

Pine Ridge Agency S.D.
Jan. 11th, 1891

Dear Joe,

Your welcome letter of the 6th came today and I was pleased to learn
that you have got the sleigh, and that the team is able to draw you
about. Glad that Julia has come to keep you company in your lonely
condition. I feel like crying out myself when I look about me and see
what dire confusion is to be seen on every hand. War at any time is not
interesting to contemplate, but when it breaks out in an Indian country
and in the winter time when weather is cold and dreary it seems less
attractive. There is little romance about it at any time.

To quote from your letter "Pine Ridge is in Peril" I must tell you in
detail the number of troops that are operating in and around this
reservation.[40] We have the Band and Head Quarters of the 1st Infty
and regiments

>   2nd Infty
>   7th Infty
>   8th Infty
>   16th Infty
>   17th Infty
>   21st Infty
>   2 Light Batteries (3 inch guns)
>   2 Howitzers
>   6th Cav
>   7th Cav
>   8th Cav
>   9th Cav
>   Indian Scouts

These troops are not all in this vicinity, but are operating in this So.
Dakota country against the Sioux. They could concentrate here if there
is a need of their services.[41]

We did not know that the Hostiles would be in today, but they have
a good many wounded, and cannot travel fast. Some of them have

come in, but the main and influential ones who decide for their tribe have not come in yet, may get here tomorrow.

Glad that Marjorie has gone back for her kindergarten again and hope she can be there every day. Now that you have your sleigh and team she can have her driver to school and return. The portrait which M[arjorie] sends of me is very life-like. I shall send some photos in which she may see her Pa-Pa.

Photographers are "thicker" about this place than you can imagine and are doing a big business. They made an appointment to take a group of this regiment today, but it blew so, they could not get a good view.

There was a service of some kind at the Catholic Mission School today. I do not think Mr. Cook held service as the Post is in so much confusion that people could not come.

I called upon Father Craft[42] the young Catholic priest who was stabbed by an Indian in the Wounded Knee fight, and he told me about it and how it happened. He had made drawings of the positions of the different factions in the contest. He told me what a struggle it is for the Indian to keep from starving. So many low whites, and squaw men are trying to get his goods, and cheat away from him on account of his ignorance and want of knowledge about how to get on in the world. Father C[raft] was glad that the military have control, and hopes they will drive out the base villains who have lived off the Indian and acted like a vampire sucking the life blood of their victims.

Capt. Pierce[43] of this 1st Reg. came today and will become the Agent for this reserve. We will wait his actions with great interest.

I send in this letter, a memoranda of my expenses to this point, which will be of use to me in collecting my Bill of Expenses to this point. The paymaster has plenty of money [but] no blanks. When the check for $100 comes I will not need any money for a while at least. It is reported that the Indians are coming in this morning, and we shall soon see the last of the hostiles.

But the time for mailing this draws nigh and I will not add any more.

Love to you, Julia and the children from

Your loving husband,
J.V. Lauderdale

Pine Ridge Agency S.D.
Monday Jan. 12th, 1891

Dear Joe,

It is a little past three o'clock in the afternoon, and I have just returned from a walk with Capt. Ewers[44] 5th Infty. You will recall Capt. E[wers] you saw him at Ft. Bliss and we rode there with the Sheldons on our way to Mexico. Capt. E[wers] has been among the Indians a great deal and understands how to deal with them. They were going to give him this Agency, but he declined it.

Capt. Pierce of the 1st, the new agent under appointment is here and called upon us. He is a large fine looking man who will command a certain amount of respect by his presence. Capt. P[ierce] has lost an eye, but the one left is quick and clear to see anything out of the way, and would serve him I hope to manage the affairs of this Agency to the satisfaction of all parties. He had charge of the San Carlos Agency in Arizona for 3 years and knows something of Indian character.

There has been a good deal of stir in camp today in view of the approach of the large body of hostiles who have agreed to treat with us. They were camped at the Catholic Mission last night and have taken a position today as near as is consistent with safety to us and themselves.

Enlisted Men's Cooking Area. Pine Ridge, South Dakota, 1891. Photograph by Clarence G. Morledge, courtesy of Rohan Collection, Nebraska State Historical Society.

Well as I was saying, Capt. Ewer and I took a walk. We went to the high ridge just back of Capt. Doherty's[45] [Dougherty] camp half a mile from this tent and from the new made trenches[46] looked out over the valley beyond and then in an angle of White Clay Creek under the lea of a rocky encircling ridge we looked upon the scattered tepees of the hostiles. A Herald reporter was there in the group taking notes of the situation. He had a Kodak camera also to shoot anything that could be shot. With a good field glass we could easily count all the tepees in sight. There were other members of the press standing about gathering items for their papers. A cool breeze was blowing, but it was tempered by the sun shining from a clear sky. Winter sunshine, it was just cool enough to bear with comfort.

There are the forces of the recent hostiles numbering about 250 tepees, and ready to listen to our overtures for peaceful relations with the whites. I hope now that the relations with this people may be more firmly established than they have ever been before, and the Army will not be called upon to do any active work to bring about amicable relations.

This gathering together of troops that cost Uncle Sam a pile of money is so unnecessary if affairs had been properly managed. But it takes experience for a people as well as for individuals to learn freedom.

Monday evening

Have had a pleasant call at Mr. Cook's the rector of the little church close to our camp. Mrs. C[ook] was born in Cambridge and is the Granddaughter of Deacon Wells of the Old White Meeting House Society. Father may have known her family. Mrs. C[ook] told me one of the grievances at this agency where a young Indian educated, and who acquired the trade of blacksmith at Carlisle School[47] holds only 2nd place in the agency shop, when his knowledge should give him first place with its better salary. The better place being given to some political underling. When the Indian parents consent to let his son go East to be educated it is that he may be able to hold a good situation when he acquires his trade. Mrs. Cook thinks that Capt. Pratt does a good

deal to estrange his pupils from their native associations, so much so
that they do not care to return and assist their Fathers and Mothers to
a better mode of life. This is certainly a grave error and should not be
allowed to exist as this idea of redeeming their people is one that
should be a prominent one to every student educated at Carlisle or
Hampton.[48] The Sioux is no common fellow, willing to be a slave to the
whites all his life but he has aspirations to be equal to his white neighbor or go as far that way as he is able. He is not allowed to vote as he
should . . .

[The remainder of this letter is missing. ed.]

                                        Pine Ridge Agency S.D.
                                        Thursday Jan. 13, 1891

Dear Joe,

I looked for a letter from you today, but did not find it. One came
from Frank which mentioned you. I am glad that you have forwarded
my random notes to Geneseo as I have not time nor sufficient compo-
sure of mind to sit down and write a fair letter concerning affairs at
this agency. Still the notes that I have sent will, if you will kindly preserve them, enable me to review the situation and some day write it
up.[49]

We have had a most beautiful day almost warm in the sun. After
attending to my sick call in this camp, I skipped off to the camp of
scouts about ten minutes walk from here to see Privates Bad Hair, Iron
Tail, and Cobb who are convalescent. Mr. Wells,[50] the interpreter, who
had an ugly cut across the bridge of his nose, returned with me to have
his wound dressed by my steward. Mr. W[ells] told me that the Brules,
and all the hostiles had come in now, and the jig is up.

Capt. Pierce sent loads of eatables to the camp of the hostiles, or
secretly hostile Indians today and I suppose they have had a feast of
fat things. It was very proper that he should do so to symbolize his
advent among them. They will probably regard him as their
"Messiah"[51] and will not have any doubt about his having come. If a
proper policy is pursued I do not see why there should be any return of

hostilities, and we may be truly thankful that much abused arm of the service—the Army has interfered with the Dept. of the Interior and driven those people out of their positions that they have too long disgraced.

All the Indians are willing to surrender their arms I am told for which they will receive a proper consideration. The Indians will deliver up the man, or men who killed Lt. Casey, also those who have committed other depredations out of the line of actual warfare. Then all will be lovely on the White Clay Creek from this time forth. So we hope and pray.

I was intending to visit the Indian boarding school with Mr. Cook this evening, but we had company in our tent and I could not get away in time. I walked down to the agency buildings and everything is quiet. It has been ration day today, and long lines of Indian men and women have waited their turn at the issue door, and I dare say they all got full measure and running over of such articles of food as they had to give them.

Did I mention that Col. Cody (Buffalo Bill) is in town, and a conspicuous figure as he rides by mounted upon a fine horse? I do not know his exact mission, but have heard that he is here in the interest of the Governor of Nebraska, and a looker on at the proceedings that are going on about us.

Miss Shepard a trained nurse sent here by Bishop Hare arrived today in the stage, and is looking after wounded Indians in the Chapel.

Wednesday Morning
Jan 14, '91

Rested better last night than night before, as there was no wind to shake our cassavas. A mule hitched near the Artillery park kept up a lively tatoo on an iron feed box, till he was assisted by a member of the guard which aroused me from my slumbers towards morning.

It was rumored last evening that Gen'l Miles had telegraphed to Washington that he had no more use for the troops. It may be true I said to Col. Bache Med. Director that just as soon as he had done with me an order sending me back to my wife and babies would be very acceptable. He replied that just as soon as he received an order to disband he should relieve me.

The Indians do not care for the presence of the troops after what they have seen of them lately.

I see a good many of the old hostile chiefs coming in to interview Gen'l Miles and the new agent.

A long line of the wagons of the 17th Infty were making their way to the supply depot. Every body feels easy as to the issue of events, and the promise for the future good behavior of the Indians seems to be assured.

One or two badly wounded soldiers in the Gen'l Hospital have died[52] which casts a gloom over that part of the agency enclosure where their tents are located.

I shall look for a letter from you this morning. I am getting behind in current news of the day, and wish you would mail me any copies of the N.Y. Times that you think will interest me. I can not get hold of any papers these days. They ask ten cents a piece for Chicago, and Omaha papers and often they do not contain any thing but sensational news.

With a great deal of love to you and the children and Julia I remain,

Your loving husband,
J.V. Lauderdale

Pine Ridge Agency
Jan 14, 1891

Dear Joe,

There are a good many people in this camp, but it is not every one that I feel like chatting with, and so I will sit me down by my lamp and scratch you a few lines. I was talking with Capt. Baldwin this evening about Ft. Davis and he told me that Dr. Skinner got our horse in a raffle, and he only cost him four dollars. Lt. Bowen[53] sold him the buggy, and one day they had hitched him to it. The animal started and ran away breaking the vehicle up, so that it was beyond repair. Dr. S[kinner] rides Fred, and had him when Captain and he were out on a practice march, and they each had a chance to ride him and liked him very much as a saddle horse.

Capt. B[aldwin] has a very high opinion of Dr. S[kinner] and thinks him above all suspicion of any irregularities of life. Says he while on the march used to receive a great many letters from his wife, and does not believe him to be bad. Does not have any very exalted opinion of Sanderson, and thinks him base enough for any slander. It may be that Skinner has turned over a new leaf since he has been at Davis. Capt. B[aldwin] says that Gen'l. Miles has ordered a private car to meet him at Rushville day after tomorrow that is the 16th when he hopes to have this Indian business in such a shape that he can entrust it to his subalterns.

Capt. B[aldwin] expects to go to Ft. Keogh overland with an escort. Capt. Ewers accompanies a body of Indians to Standing Rock agency, and Capt. Pierce will retain charge at this Agency. Baldwin says they will keep a large body of troops here this winter to prevent any more uprisings among the Indians.

There have been quite a good number of Doctors in Camp today. Dr. Eddy that we saw in San Antonio, Leonard Wood,[54] Spencer,[55] Kane,[56] Appel[57] (a brother of the Dr. we know). There are eighteen doctors in, and at the near camps I rank No. 4 in the list.

Thursday Jan 15; It is cold and misty this morning and frost gathers on all objects—the cords of our tent are covered with a delicate fringe. I walked down to the Gen'l Hospital with Dr. Hartsuff,[58] and we went to take a look at the English Field equipment sent out by Dr. Vollum.[59] You know Dr. V[ollum] was in Eng[land] last spring, and saw something there which took his fancy, and he brot it over and now it is here for the instruction of our Doctors. It consists of twelve panniers each made of a frame of wicker work covered with raw hide, and then divided into wooden compartments & drawers for the medicine, dressings, and all the utensils that can be needed in a fully equipped field hospital.

All the morning the late hostile Indians have been stringing along the hillside with their horses, and wagons, families, and will take a position over against the friendlies. They have moved from the position I saw them first while with Capt. Ewers, and will now go thro with

Lt. Colonel and Surgeon Edward P. Vollum. Photograph courtesy United States Army Military History Institute.

the ceremony of turning in their arms for which they will receive checks, or their money value. I shall hope for a letter today. The stage just drove by our Camp.

Love to you and the children and Aunt Julia from,

Your loving husband,
J.V. Lauderdale

Pine Ridge Agency
Thursday Jan. 15, 1891

Dear Joe,

Your letter of the 10th inst. containing the check was handed me today. I have received three letters all told. The affair at Presidio—the advent of Ed Lauderdale Ellis[60] must have been an event of no ordinary moment on the Pacific Coast, and of course the parents may not be blamed if they go into rapture over it. It is their way of doing things.

I am glad to learn that Lady[61] is recovering from her lameness, and that you can get some use of the sleigh. Keep it agoing every day as the team has not had its share of duty during those days when good sleighing was abundant, and we had nothing to ride in.

I assure you that I shall not linger here one hour longer than I am obligated to when the order comes to disband.

What induced you to give Vance Cod Liver Oil? Sweet cream will do him more good, and is more digestible. I do not blame V[ance] for not taking the nauseous dose.

We have had a beautiful day this afternoon, it has been bright and sunshine has flooded the land. After standing for my picture with a group of the officers of the 1st I took a walk over to the camp of the 7th Cavalry, and called upon Dr. Hoff,[62] and found him seated in his little wall tent pouring over his books. He was as snug as a bug in a rug, and we had a very nice visit. Dr. H[off] told me all about Stewd Hill whom he has known for some time. Dr. said he visited Oswego once upon a time, and was the guest of an old college friend viz Mr. John Mott the same young gentleman who called upon you most likely. Dr. H[off] is a very thorough going officer and will have a good long report to make of the campaign which seems now about to close. Dr. [Hoff] is so unlike his father. He is a nephew of Dr. Van Reusiler [Rensellaer] of the Episcopal Church, and his manner is quite clerical. He could, with little fixing up pass himself off for an Episcopal rector, or lay reader.

Friday Morning Jan. 16

The late hostiles have surrendered at least a portion of their arms and are encamped in sight of the Agency, over against the ridge to the south of the Agency buildings.

The day is beautiful, with a little wind, just enough to carry the dust about, that the wheels and hoofs raise into the air. I do not know what the next move will be. No bulletins are sent and one has to get information on the droppings that fall from the office table of the Commanding General, and which is passed from mouth to mouth, and from ear to ear. The hostiles visit the camp, and their wounded friends in the Chapel. Every thing seems to be serene. I wish the troops were all marching home and I was on my way too. But we must wait-wait-wait-with patience for this great multitude of soldiers and Indians to scatter. It is not yet settled when each will go, and we must wait for the morning. It takes time and deliberation and those low down in rank must wait for their Seniors.

I see a good many officers and soldiers from neighboring commands coming and going and exchanging "howdys'," with each other and making new acquaintances. Wishing it was all settled, I remain

Your loving husband,
J.V. Lauderdale

Pine Ridge Agency S.D.
Jan 16th 1891

Dear Joe,
I was glad to get yours of last Sunday today, one came also yesterday with the check. I do not know Greenleaf, but I think he saw my name

General Charles R. Greenleaf. Photograph courtesy of the Prints and Photographs Collection, History of Medicine Division, National Library of Medicine, Bethesda, Maryland.

on the Leave of Absence list, and concluded to send me. I think my self that it would be well for him to take some of his own medicine.

I hope you will have more snow soon so that you may continue to get about comfortably. We have cloudless skies and today a mild temperature. There was considerable dust being swept through the air which is not agreeable to campers out.

So you have placed Vance on Millins food! I hope he will do well on it. I hope he has not gone back on oatmeal?

I shall not become so enamored of a tent that I will sigh for it when I return to a civilized abode. Glad that Rev. Mr. Swift called. I think him a lovely little man with a big heart.

I have had several letters from Frank two I think. You may send her any notes, but as they are but notes I want them preserved for future reference.

The Fortnightly Club must wait till I return to Oswego. I do not care for the honor without enjoying some of the advantages of membership.

I will preserve the address of Mrs. Kilduff. But in going East, it is not necessary to go through Omaha. The Missouri Valley Junction south offers a shorter cut.

I was in the N.W. Photographers Studio today, and one of the artists gave me a proof of a group of the 1st Infantry, as it is but a proof it will not bear the light, but if you open it in a dark room you may get a glimpse of our mess mates.

No. 1 Capt. [John J.] O'Connell who brot in Young Man[63]
No. 2 Capt. [Daniel F. Callinan] Caliman a poor sick man whom I sent
   off today on a Sick Leave
No. 3 Capt. [Francis E.] Pierce the New Agent
4 Dr. Gardner (uncle of Dr. Harris) & loves whiskey too well
5 Col. [William R.] Shafter—Not altogether to my fancy
6 Lt. Col. [James S. Casey] Cassey a quite old gentleman
7 Capt. [William E.] Doherty [Dougherty] a regular Irish Soldier and
   quite agreeable
8 Capt. [Robert G.] Armstrong a gentleman
9 Lt. Sims
10 " Markham

11 " [Frank L.] Winn
12 " [John Stanford Jr.] Mason
13 " [Captain Thomas H.] Barry
14 An Officer of the Cloman [Second Lieutenant Sydney A. Cloman]
15 Lt. [Captain Marion P.] Maus
16 Lt. [Charles G.] Starr Regt Q.M.
17 Lt. [Frederic A.] Tripp
18 Lt. [Frank de L.] Carrington Adjt.
19 Lt.[Louis P.] Bryant
20 Yours truly[64]
I shall have some permanent views of the above and others to bring home.

I was conversing with one of the soldiers employed in the agency shop and was surprised to learn with what contempt they hold the Indian employees in this shop. Those who have been taught at Carlisle to do saddlery work are not properly rewarded for their labor, and the white men get the lion's share of the pay for the work done there, because they are the friends of rascally politicians and return to the same political demagogues a part of their earnings. Another instance when the Indian should have the pay instead of the white employee.

Officers of the First U.S. Infantry, Pine Ridge, South Dakota, January 1891. (Note John V. Lauderdale second from right standing.) Photograph courtesy of The Denver Public Library, Western History Department.

I see that Dr. Gardner goes and leaves me the ranking Medical Officer is just as well. He drinks too much, and does not do anything so may as well be off for he is only a nuisance to the rest of us. He thinks that he is of great importance the little old toper. Will not add more. A beautiful day lovely as Texas winter. Love to you and the children and Julia from

Your loving husband,
J.V. Lauderdale

Pine Ridge Agency S.D.
Jan. 17th 1891

Dear Joe,

We have had a lovely winter day. There has been a large multitude of Indian soldiers and half breeds wandering about, but everybody's face wore more the appearance of content than hitherto.

I called in at the Gen'l Hospital and found the cases doing fairly well. There are thirteen soldiers still in hospital, not all however due to the recent battle. There are about a dozen cases remaining among the Indian prisoners in the Chapel. The first order has been issued looking like disbanding the Army. A dozen or so of the Hospital Corps are ordered back to their Posts, as they are not wanted here any longer and are only in the way. This is the beginning of disbanding, and I shall be ready at a moment's notice to comply with an order sending me East.

Many of the distinguished hostile chiefs have been in and about the Post today, and I think are glad that the trouble is over. As they have had the worst of it.

An old acquaitance among the photographers made his appearance today Mr. Cross,[65] who made the group at Ft. Sully—the small sterographic pictures. He gave me view that he made at this Agency two years ago showing the place in the quiet times of peace. Mr. C[ross] wishes to get some of the Gen'l Officers, as well as views of the place in its changed condition.

It is ordered that the First Infty will return to California sooner or later. But the best thing which came last night is an order sending all

Grand Council of Hostile and Friendly Sioux Indian Chiefs at Pine Ridge Agency S.D. Jan 17th 1891

Copyrighted Jan 30th 1891 by the North Western Photo Co. Chadron Neb.

Chief Young Man Afraid of his Horses talking

Surrender at Pine Ridge, 17 January 1891. Photograph courtesy of the Nebraska State Historical Society.

Officers who do not think themselves able to join in the duties of active hostilities before a retiring board. Major Dr. G[ardner] you remember has said from the first that he could not do active field service, and today an order came relieving him from duty with this Regiment. G[ardner] has made long and eloquent complaints of his rheumatism and neuralgia. Everyone knows that his ills are due to liquor. In view of the order relieving him from his duty I hope there may come another order sending him before a Retiring Board, as his disease is one which I do not believe to be due to the exigencies of the service. It is due the younger members of the Corps that he should be made an example of Dr. Hartsuff says he should have charges preferred against him. I related an outline of his case to Med. Director Bache and he smiled behind his spectacles. I do not know as anything will be done, but I think a good case could be made out of it.

Sunday Noon Jan 18th

At 11 o'clock the Chapel bell rang out clear and musical and I went over to Mr. Cook's house where a few of the faithful to the number of twenty Indians of both sexes met for religious worship. Mr. Cook plays the melodeon and sings and then reads the Episcopal English service. There seems to be a general participation by the audience in the service. The address is in Dakota and delivered by Mr. C[ook] with true apostolic spirit, and is listened to attentively to the close. After the offertory follows the benediction. I think if it was not for the good council given in these churches, in keeping a large part of the tribe in a friendly state, our task of subduing the turbulent spirits would have been a far greater one.

It is a lovely day. I wish you were here to take a walk with me about, and see what an Army we have camped about us, and then come to our dining tent and take lunch with us. With a great deal of love to you and the children and Aunt Julia. I remain,

> Your loving husband,
> J.V. Lauderdale

> Camp Pine Ridge Agency
> Sunday Jan. 18, 1891

Dear Joe,

My heart is made glad today by receiving yours of the 13th inst. It was written after you had just returned from a sleigh ride, and reaches me in my tent with the door wide open and a warm sun shining down upon us. I have also a letter from Frank, containing a clipping from the World written by our Miss Goodale.

Capt. Dougherty just whispered to me that the man who has been furnishing the horses with which to mount our Infantry has been sent for to come and take away his herd as we have no further use for them. This looks like closing out of this war business, which also pleases me.

Medical Department Ambulance ca. 1880s. Drawing courtesy of James W. Wengert, M.D., Omaha, Nebraska.

An ambulance "A Red Cross" just drove up in front of the little Chapel across the street with a wounded squaw who has come in, and given herself up for treatment. A crowd of Soldiers gathers about to do any thing for the poor creature. Dr. Kilborne just left my tent to look after her.[66] Wouldn't you think that the Indians who saw so much done for their wounded would be convinced that there is a kindly spirit among the pale-faces beneath all their stern demeanor when urged on to war and its deadly doings?

Later I heard that the above woman was of a party out hunting and were fired into by cowboys, with intent to kill and she survival [survived] the attempt at murder.

One of our Officers was telling how the cowboys drive their horses onto the Indian Reservations so as to avoid paying taxes on them, thus imposing on the natives and cheating government of its just dues.

Monday Morning.

The killing of the above party is causing much excitement in Army circles and will delay the settlement of the Indian question. If an Indian life is not safe from cowboy violence and murder then we cannot expect to make any binding promises with these people. I think Gen'l. Miles will do everything in his power to ferret out the miscontent, and I believe if we had him in our hands we would suspend him from the cross trees of the flag staff. So great is the indignation felt towards the fiend who did this base act.

I saw Capt. Wells[67] this morning. He had just come in from his detachment. Mrs. W[ells] you remember at Ft. Clark who showed us the Mexican spoons . . .

I called on Gen'l. Brooke this morning. He is our alternate Comdg General if Gen'l. Miles goes. But Gen'l. M[iles] will not leave till this business is settled.

Last evening our troop broke up a faro bank and its roulette dealings. I saw the green furniture at Col. Shafter's tent door this morning. So you see we are looking after the morals of the Pine Ridgers, and clearing out the gamblers.[68]

I hope you will send me the N.Y. Times after you read them as they may contain some items that I do not see in the Chicago Inter Ocean, the paper I purchase and read daily. I have nothing new to tell you. I am feeling pretty well and hope you and the children are quite well and happy. With a great deal of love to you and Julia I remain,

Your loving husband,

J.V. Lauderdale

P.S. You must send Frank any notes that you think will interest her or Father as I have not time to write you both.

J.L.

Pine Ridge Agency
Jan. 19, 1891

Dear Joe,

I went down to Head Quarters this morning, and when I met Dr.
Bache he made this dubious remark "There has been a hitch in proceedings" and things are not moving as fast as we expected. The arrival
of the wounded woman (Indian) yesterday with the story that she and
her party had been almost totally annihilated by cowboys, and she
with two bad wounds had made her way towards this Agency after several days' journey was so thrilling and made us feel like annihilating
the bad cowboy element before completing the settlement of the Indian
troubles, and we felt our own shirts must be clean if we expect to treat
with our Indians.

Gen'l. Miles will use his utmost endeavors to ferret out this das-
tardly crime if it takes all winter and will have the offender brot to
answer for his reckless killing of Indians. There is too much of the bad
cowboy element in this country and it is working against peaceful
negotiations. If we can not keep our cowboys from killing Indians,
they need not expect us to protect them when in danger. We are not
going to carry on a war of extermination of Indians for all the cowboys
and settlers for we do not believe it to be right to do so. But rather
preserve peace between them. This is Gen'l. Miles plan, and he will
carry it out too.

If it takes a little longer time to settle these Indian troubles on a true
basis it will not be time thrown away. While it is not pleasant for us in
the Army to be living in tents away from our families, we may be able
by a longer residence among the Indians enable the latter to see that we
are their friends and will defend them at all hazards against the bad
white man who has no doubt made all this trouble.

I walked with Dr. B[ache] and called upon Gen'l. Brooke who has
recently returned to the Agency from duty at one of the outlying
camps. I also met Col. Ofley[69] of the 17th Infty.

Capt. Baldwin came over and dined at our mess this evening, and he
and Col. Shafter ran over Civil War reminiscences of times when they

fought a more determined and manly foe than we have to deal with now. Not time to complete this.

Love to all,

Yours lovingly,
J.V. Lauderdale

Pine Ridge Agency
Tuesday Jan. 20th, 1891

Dear Joe,

We have had a dusty disagreeable day. I repaired to the room of the Photographers at an early hour to see what kind of picture he had developed for me. You know I found that I could take his camera and reduce his 5 X 8 negatives to a lantern size. I placed a picture of Gen'l. Miles and his staff in the window and made an exposure, which he developed for me and it makes a very good positive for a lantern slide. I had made others today which I hope will turn out equally good.

Major Gardner was not so ill, that he could not ride down to the battle field at Wounded Knee with two ladies, one a teacher here, and the other a Mrs. Dean[70] a correspondent of a Chicago paper who is out here to write up the account of the late battle.

Orders have come for the Battery of Artillery to move out of camp about two miles tomorrow which means a start toward Rushville, and ultimately to their home at Ft. Riley.

It is reported today that the cowboys who killed the Indian party have been heard from and that they did not conceal their deed, but published the fact in the papers. We will see what will come of it. The murderers should be punished for their cowardly conduct.

Wednesday Jan. 21

A movement out has been going on all morning among the Battery people. Since breakfast miles, and miles of troops have been passing our camp in route to the new camping station. The Ninth Cavalry under Colonel Henry[71] headed the column, and the colored boys rode by in fine spirits, and you know colored troops always fall into such comical attitudes that they generally cause a ripple of laughter all along their route. It was better than Forepaughs Circus to watch them. Tell David[72] he should have been here to see them.

Mr. Mallory tells me that each team used in transporting baggage costs U.S. $11. Eleven dollars a day. What a big bill of expenses will be footed up as the cost of this uprising among these poor Sioux, whom we have been depriving of their just dues thro the plundering deeds of the Interior (Indian Ring) Dept. It would have been cheaper to gather up these tribes and board them at the Fifth Ave. Hotel than to send the Army out on the plains of Dakota and fight them, or as we have done shown them what we can do. The Indians in their tepees all about the Agency must rejoice that our Army has not annihilated them. But they are our people and we do not wish to kill them if we can help them to help themselves.

Lt. Chamberlin (Johnnie)[73] tells me that he is under orders to return to his station in Washington, but says he is in no hurry to go. But I think will go when his battery reaches Rushville.

It is somewhat windy again today, and the dust is flying all over everything. It began snowing after breakfast but it has all disappeared from sight in the dry earth and atmosphere

With much love to you and the family I remain,

Your loving husband,
J.V. Lauderdale

Pine Ridge Agency
Jan. 21, 1891

Dear Joe,

Yours and Marjorie's letters of the 16th inst came duly to my hand today, and I am glad to know that you are well and comfortable. Not withstanding the cold weather you are experiencing. I used to shut the doors opening into the hall, and then the heat from the furnace would warm both rooms, the parlor, and bedroom.

Marjorie tells me in her letter that the plumber is at work in the bathroom. I hope that he is putting in the new porcelain tub. Capt.

Baldwin wishes to be remembered to you and Marjorie. I must show him M[arjorie]'s letter. If I am not much mistaken Capt. B[aldwin] is calling on Col. Shafter in the next tent. I asked the Captain who has the ear of Gen'l. Miles how things are getting on and he said "very well." But I get greatly out of patience sometimes waiting for this business to close and let us go to our homes.

Major Gardner is anxious to get away and I am jealous of him as he is only playing he is sick, and can not do full duty. Tonight he said his wife had a bad cold, and he wanted to go back to Cal. If he gets away and I have to stay I feel as if I shall resign my Commission.

I do not like being detained anytime, now that the emergency is over. Why we have more Doctors than patients, and have little to do at any time. This makes the time hang heavy.

I see that six men of the Hospital Corps have been ordered to their Posts and have left this Post which is an earnest [sign] that disbanding is begun. Tomorrow forenoon they are to have a grand review of the troops down the Rushville road about two miles from here. I do not know whether I shall go and see it or not. If I can get a mount I may go.

I can not tell you when they will let me go. No one of the Doctors has been released as yet. Dr. Hartsuff intimated to me that I would have to stay a while. I am a great mind to make a special application to be released. It is true that I never have done as much field duty as a great many in all my Army life, and they may think that as they have got me out here they will keep me a while. The Army is a bad place for one who has to do what he does not wish to. I sometimes think I will throw up my commission, and the prospect of my retired pay for the sake of having my own way, but that would not be as well for you and the children at this time of my life. I am not alone in this dilemma. There are several score of Officers who would like to go to their several homes as well as myself, but who continue doing their duty uncomplainingly, and so I suffer to stick it out.

The mail closes at this time and I will send you my love to you and the children.

Your loving husband,
J.V. Lauderdale

Pine Ridge Agency S.D.
Thursday Jan. 22, 1891

Dear Joe,

It was reported yesterday that there would be a review of the troops by Gen'l. Miles, and everybody who had a mount and those who had not, tried to get to see it. It was held down on the Rushville road about two miles from the Agency. I could have had a pony to ride, but it was cold and I did not care to ride a horse, unless I am obligated to, as it lames me so that I do not get over it for a few days.

I saw Dr. Hartsuff and he said he thot he could get a Red Cross Ambulance, and with a Q.M. team we could ride down to the place of review. Later Dr. H[artstuff] called upon Dr. Bache, Med. Director and asked for an ambulance, and was refused it so Dr. H[artstuff] said that he thot he would stay at home. I looked about for some way to ride and observed Mr. Smith one of the Catechists at Mr. Cook's hitching up his team and accosting him asked him which way he was going. He replied that he was going to drive down to Rushville, and if I wished would be happy to take me down to the review. A Mr. Keith who is one of the teachers at Wounded Knee Post School got in and rode with us. We rode by the Indian village with its cluster of tepees, and at length came to the long crest from which we had a view of the Army stretching away for two miles. About the time we got to the center of the line the column began to move.

Old Gen'l. Forsyth[74] had just been out on the hill looking over the scene but dismounted, poor man he is still deprived of Command,[75] and is only a looker on at parades. Gen'l. Carr[76] is in command of the Cavalry Brigade, and Col. Wheaton[77] of the Infantry. I did not wait to see more than the moving of the vast Army but Mr. K[eith] and I began our march back to the Agency. About the time the battalion of Scouts under Lt. Taylor[78] passed us.

As we walked homeward our boys of the 1st Infty (4 companies) passed us. As we were ascending a little hill we were passed by Dr. Eastman (Indian Dr.) and his fiancee Miss Elaine Goodale who were in a top buggy with two horses and had just come from witnessing the review of the troops.

"General Miles' Cavalry At Pine Ridge" on review, by Frederic Remington.
22 January 1891. Drawing courtesy Frederic Remington Art Museum,
Ogdensburg, New York.

"General Miles' Cavalry At Pine Ridge" on review, by Frederic Remington.
22 January 1891. Drawing courtesy Frederic Remington Art Museum,
Ogdensburg, New York.

Dr. (Maj. Gardner) started for home this evening. He might as well be away for all the good he does—a chronic toper who says he cannot ride a horse. It would be the best for the service if such Drs. could go before a retiring board and ship out. But he is a very social fellow, and all who have a failing in the same direction don't like to cast the first stone at him and so he is allowed to go back to his post.

I have a letter from Frank with news from home. Lt. Chamberlin [left] this evening for Washington having finished his short campaign inside of ten days

Friday Jan. 23rd

Well my dear I have got to stay a month longer, or until the whole business of caring for the sick is closed. I cannot get around it unless I resign my commission, and I presume you will object to my doing that.

Major Gardner left last night because he was utterly worthless. Col. Shafter said his own phrascology he "would not give him hell room for all he did." Said he was all the time complaining of his stomach which he kept well warmed with whiskey. Dr. Hartsuff advised him to prefer charges against him, I wish he would do so.

There will be the 1st Reg. Infty Band and Hd Qtrs command who will occupy the agency buildings—at least the Officers will have rooms. I will be in full charge of Medical matters, with the assistance of Dr. Cabell,[79] and Kane. There will be a regiment of mounted troops the 9th Cav. Col. Henry and Stafford[80] (the colored reg.) and the company of Indian Scouts who will do all the outpost duty about the Agency. There is no prospect of any active service, but these troops are left to close up matters, and get order out of confusion. I would prefer to return home today, but if you can get along without me for another month, I think I can be able to get away then. I hope all will be just as well with you.

With a great deal of love to you and the children and Aunt Julia. I remain,

Your loving husband,
J.V. Lauderdale

Pine Ridge Agency
Friday Jan. 23, 1891

Dear Joe,

So, I am booked for a longer stay here. I could not prevent it unless I absolutely refused to stay, and that you know would involve me in disgrace, which I believe you would not have me do. After Maj. Gardner left this Regiment I am the only Officer left with it. Capt. Gardner[81] has to go with the wounded to Ft. Riley tomorrow. Two Officers, Drs. Cabell and Kane are with the 9th Cavalry about two miles away and will do all the field service. Dr. Hartsuff the Officer ranking next to Bache the Medical Director turns over such of his medicines as I need, and returns with the 2nd Infantry to his post at Fort Omaha. He has been out here since the 20th of November. There will be but a very few cases in [the] Hospital and so not much for me to do. If the Indians behave themselves we will all break up and go in a short time. Gen'l. Miles is here yet.

Capt. Baldwin is quite sick today. He rode out with Gen'l. M[iles] to the review yesterday, and took cold which settled in his bones and he has been in his bed all day. I read him your letter and showed him Marjorie's letter and it pleased him very much.

Saturday Morning

As I lay last night on my pillow, I planned all kinds of complaining letters to the Adjt. Gen'l for sending me out here and now for keeping me here a day after the "strife" is over. But Mallory my tent mate, and nearly everybody else, but the people of the 1st Infty, cannot sympathize with me as they have all been here fully two months. While I have not completed one month yet. And they have wives and children at home who long to see them as much as I wish to see mine. The people of the 1st Infty who are here from California would not stay a day longer if they could help themselves.

Col Henry is in command of the colored regiment, and he hangs on although Mrs. H[enry] who is in Omaha I dare say would like him to

Company K of the Ninth U.S. Cavalry at Pine Ridge, 1891. Photograph courtesy of the Nebraska State Historical Society.

come home. Col. Henry says that he lives on his nerve and supposes he will remain here till next June when the crops begin to grow. The Cavalry are always kept in the field when other troops are stationed in Posts.

To refer to your letter, I am sorry for poor Marjorie that she is so lonely. I hope you can keep Julia with you for a while longer. If the sleighing is good you can enjoy the going about. We want to get the full worth of the sleigh out of it. This is the pleasantest place I ever saw for a winter climate, unless it is Texas.

I guess you paid all my pledges at Grace Church correctly. You may send me another check for my signature, so that you can pay the bills for January with it.

Speaking of Capt. Powell,[82] Capt. Gardner said last evening that "he is a pig" referring to his habit of getting all he can out of Government. That was a good joke on Dr. Hill and Dr. Powell.

I wish you would paint Marjorie's chest with Tr Iodine a thin solution, and see if that will relieve her chest trouble. I am sure a good article of Cod Liver Oil Emulsion such as you can find at Butlers may be good for her, but plenty of sweet cream for her diet will also do her a heap of good. I hope that Seymour will be able to see his way out of the woods into something to his advantage.

I am glad to get all the papers you have to send me. I enjoy the Harpers Weekly, and all the other papers, N.Y. Times, Oswego Times, and all. Am quite busy this morning, and will not add more but my love to you and the children and Aunt Julia.

Your loving husband,
J.V. Lauderdale

Pine Ridge Agency
Jan. 24, 1891

Dear Joe,
I called on Capt. Baldwin this evening and find him pretty comfortable. I am very glad that it was nothing more than a case of over doing himself on a cold day, and throwing himself into a chill by not taking due care of himself. Let me tell you how he is situated. He is all alone in a large Sibley tent. Has a straw tick filled and some blankets upon that. A pillow, for his head and blankets, and a piece of old canvass over him. His tent is heated with a box stove. He has a little table, and a lamp upon it, a water pail, and basin and cup and some kind of camp chairs. A revolver lies on a box near his bed which is stretched at full length upon the ground.

This afternoon and during all the day the wind blew and the dust rose and was swept over the country in a frightful manner. It was worse than you ever saw at Ft. Davis.

Dr. Gandy[83] who is with one of the Regiments and was snatched up from a leave of absence was here today and called upon me. He goes with troops to Ft. Niobrarra, and when he reaches that point will turn over his box and return to his leave of absence again.

I had a call from Lt. Robert Gelty, who is in command of a company of scouts. I used to know him at Ft. Hamilton when he was just thinking of going to West Point.

Sunday Morning Jan. 25

Capt. B[aldwin] is much better this morning. Gen'l. Miles came in his tent while I was there, and says you are a fine fellow to get sick. Gen'l. M[iles] is not a man of many words. He reminds me very much in looks and dress of some actor—John McCullough—he wears rather fancy leggins and some times it is almost the black stockings and it would need only the knee buttons and shoe buckles to give him an old time knickerbocker look. Has a blond face and no hair on his face now. They leave tomorrow.

I think it an outrage that I am detained here, but no one looks at it as I do for they have been here twice as long as I have. If I was sure of my living, I would tender my resignation. I have just written Gen'l. Sutherland[84] a personal note asking that I be relieved as soon as possible. The people of this Regt of course want me to stay till they go. I want to go on general principles, and for your sake. I have no other reason. You need not tell anyone that I want to go back for they will at once conclude that I am no soldier.

One of the Corps [Hospital Corps] from Detroit tells me that they are having a siege of diphtheria at Ft. Wayne and that Mamie Smith is very sick with it. You know she has always had a bad throat and now it is very bad. Sorry for them but the Steward says it is due to bad sewerage, and unhealthy surroundings.

They are busy arranging my Hospital today and have turned to a few of the sick that could not be sent away.

Dr. Bradley[85] and I will look after them, and when things are settled will not probably have a very heavy task if the weather continues good.

No more at this time from

Your loving husband,
J.V. Lauderdale

Pine Ridge Agency S.D.
Sunday Jan. 25, 1891

Dear Joe,

I have just been down to the Agency buildings to look after matters in the new Post Hospital. I have placed the single ward under the charge of my young colleague Dr. Bradley, who will remain on duty with me for a time. I shall have a general oversight of medical matters, will attend sick call and attend to other executive business which may be required.

I was called in to see the Post Trader's wife who is suffering from a sore throat. She is a Mrs. Asa [Asay][86] probably of Jewish name. These people have their rooms lined with Indian curios of all kinds. There is a strange mingling of oil paintings, curios, tapestry, bric-a-brac, and an upright piano. Navajo blankets, bead[ed] Ute shirts and Indian porcupine work festoon the furniture and walls.

All the stores are closed today, and there are not so many Indians hanging about the Post as on other days.

This evening at half past four I answered the summons of the Chapel bell and attended the evening services at Mr. Cook's house. It was mostly in Sioux, but I had the Episcopal prayer book and could follow a portion of it. The songs were also in Dakota, but the music was English. One of the little boys that was shot in the face at Wounded Knee was at the service, and he sat with his head all bound up quite attentive to the services of Mr. Cook. I think if Mr. Crocker had been there he would have taken it all in as he made some pretension to a knowledge of that language.

The Catechists, or lay readers, well dressed Sioux do the heavy singing and responding in the preliminary service. It shows how the power of the Gospel has turned the hearts of these barbarians, and made them to become orderly citizens of this country who should be allowed to vote.

Just at this time, I hear shouts of Indian lads mingled with the barking of dogs that are so numerous about the tepees in the village just over the hill. The Gospel has not reached them yet, and for this reason they have been the victims of an insurrection which came very near wiping them out of existence.

I received a little pamphlet from Bishop Hare today in which he goes over the causes that have led to the recent trouble. I will send it to you for your perusal, and you may send it to Father. I wish it again for future reference.

Colonel Guy V. Henry, Commanding Officer Ninth U. S. Cavalry. Taken at the Rifle Range in Bellevue, Nebraska, 1888. Photograph, courtesy of the United States Army Military History Institute.

Monday Morning Jan. 26

There is great commotion in the Agency this morning in view of the departure of Gen'l. Miles' Staff and about forty Indians mostly Brules who go to Chicago,[87] and will there be taken care of. It is on the whole cheaper to feed and fete these people than to fight them, and so the General will take them home with him.

I was talking with Col. Henry who is in command of the 9th Cavalry left behind, and he says that it is an outrage that he should be left and the 6th Cavalry ordered to their Posts. The Colonel and I sympathize with each other on our being left. Col. H[enry] said privately that he's a great mind to turn Indian and stay here all the time and if he does will get up an insurrection that will not be so easily put down as the late one. But this is between ourselves and must not be divulged.

I will not send more today but my love to you and the children from

Your loving husband.

J.V. Lauderdale

Pine Ridge Agency S.D.
Jan. 26th, 1891

Dear Joe,

Yours of the 21st came after my letter had gone to the office. I read M[arjorie]'s letter about the pipe in the parade bursting. She speaks of sleigh riding but I read in the papers of freshets in the Hudson, and Mohawk country and I expect that you may have lost your fine snow by this time, though I hope not, as is such a nice way of getting around the city. Am glad that you find large coal more economical, and I wish you would buy more of it as you need it.

We have had a great day for this Agency the departure of Gen'l. Miles with his staff and about Forty Indians. The General rode his horse out of town. The staff were in carriages, spring wagons, and the Indians were riding in lumber wagons with plenty of hay to sit upon. Crowds of woman and children, the families of the Indians, stood about and kept up a kind of low singing or warbling as they always do when they are taking leave of their friends. But every body seemed to be pleased with the arrangements, and today many of the Indians have turned their faces toward their homes and other places where they usually set up their tepees. Capt. Ewers will try to get off day after tomorrow with his Indians for Standing Rock. I shall furnish him with a package of medicine to use as necessary on the road.

I have just come from the Hospital where I left Act. Steward Appel. He showed me some fine specimens of onyx which he obtained in old Mexico. He gave me a very pretty specimen of selenite which I will add to my collection. My Stewards, and members of the Corps to the number of seven have got the Hospital in pretty good shape, and the patients who are under Dr. Bradley's immediate care are pretty comfortable. They are more comfortable in a house than they were in tents.

Capt. Pierce the newly appointed Agent continues ill, and one of the Officers of this Regt attends to his duties.

Dr. Hartsuff who was in charge of the General Hospital and Dr. Kilborne who has been attending to the wounded in the Chapel go tomorrow. Most of the Indian wounded either died or have left there because they wanted to be with their friends. Indians do not make good patients as they refuse to have such surgical aid as could be given them if they would submit to it under aether [ether]. In looking over Dr. Kilborne's work, I think he might do better work although he may not get much thanks for it. But he could make a reputation for himself, and his profession among these people.

Tuesday Jan. 27th, Noon

I have just been examining some Indians for the mounted police force and see some strange marks upon their bodies where they have been scarified by the Medicine Men.

In considerable of a hurry I remain,

Your loving husband,
J.V. Lauderdale

P. S. Plenty of snow this morning. J.V.L.

Pine Ridge Agency S.D.
Jan. 27th, 1891

Dear Joe,

Last night we had a fall of six inches of snow and it has lain quietly upon the surface of the ground. So that instead of shuffling around in sand, we have been stumping around in clean white snow almost the color of our white Sibley tents. It has changed the whole aspect of nature. It is not very cold, and we think it a great blessing to have the dirt covered up.

Three of the Doctors; Hartsuff, Gibson, and Kilborne, took their departure today for their respective Posts. Bradley, and I alone are left at this Post. Drs. Cabell and Kane are about six miles out in Col. Henry's camp. Dr. Eastman the Indian doctor, and those above, constitute the Medical faculty at this time.

Capt. Armstrong[88] told me that he saw in the Personal of the Army & Navy Journal that I am expected soon to return to Ft. Ontario. But you must never put any confidence in those reports as I am not aware that any order has been issued yet for my return. They have got a sober doctor, in the place of a whiskey bibber, and they do not care to make any change. If Gardner had not played sick, but attended to his duty my occupation here would also be at an end and I would be on my way East. They have sent off two or three poor sticks, and kept enough good men to look after the sick of the troops remaining. Dr. Ives is not much of a doctor. He was assigned to some duty with the Indian prisoners, but he did not attend to his duty very closely, and did not make a reputation. He was the caterer of the Gen'l Mess, and contracted with some woman to make fresh biscuits every day. He was to furnish the flour. When she finished her work she brot in a bill of $60. Sixty dollars. The members would not pay but Fifteen dollars. She brot a bill against poor Ives for the balance.

We have a splendid mess, chicken or turkey, with a variety of other meats at every meal. Clean napkins every day, and good cooking of wholesome articles without any attempts at cakes, or pastry. Good funnel cakes, and such articles as I would find at home. Cost not over and less than a dollar a day. Attentive soldier waiters.

If I should be ordered to return with the 1st Infty to California would you object? I should get more mileage, besides seeing something of the country. I would not remain there but a day or two. You need not think I will ask to go, but should I be ordered and could not get out of it the trip there and return to Ft. Ontario would be a good way to end this campaign. You may be sure I will take the first chance if it is to go to Ft. Ontario [rather] than prolong my absence from home.

Captain and Assistant Surgeon Francis J. Ives. Photograph courtesy of the Prints and Photographs Collection, History of Medicine Division, National Library of Medicine, Bethesda, Maryland.

Dr. Eastman and I have been busy today examining Indian Scouts, or Mounted Police they call them. Dr. E[astman] did the talking, and I did the examining, we passed Seventy Nine. We found a good many that engaged in the Sun Dance in times past, and had their manly breasts scarred with the old cicatrices of the loops of raw hide which supported their bodies during those severe ordeals.[89]

Some had their arms covered with small elevations along the outer aspects as if the skin had been pierced with a needle and caught in what surgeons would call a harelip suture. Very few were tattooed, one had his name "Red Nest"[90] in India ink on his forearm. The order is to enlist a hundred of these Indians and they will have a chance to practice some of their arts of war, in preserving the peace.

With love to all.

Your loving husband,
J.V. Lauderdale

Pine Ridge Agency S.D.
Wed. Jan. 28th, 1891

Dear Joe,

Your good letter of the 23rd came today. I rec'd one from Frank also of [the] same date. Send to Ed for any money you may need to pay current expenses. I am so surprised that Marjorie does not get well of her cough. She seems to be in such good general health always. I wonder if it would not be well to put her in a sleeping bay, so that she shall keep the clothing over her all night, instead of lying so much of the time with nothing on but her sleeping gown?

And the Steward has the gout? Good for him I suppose it is the high living! As for Molloy he is a hard case to manage as he is so fond of going to town and at times gets off the track.

As I have said we have plenty of snow, and I wish you could drive into our camp with your ponies and sleigh and take me out for a ride. I hope the storms you have had of late will not take off your snow and put an end to the sleighing.

I am sorry that poor Julia is a prisoner, literally a prisoner of war, for if it had not been for this Sioux war, I presume she would have returned to Brooklyn by this time. We must make good her losses, and perhaps pay her way as she is your companion and gives her time.

Frank says Walter[91] has gone to Fla. Asks if any of the Officers have their wives with them? She thinks you would like it out here. She wishes me to send her some memento of the war. I will see what I can find and send to her.

The men began clearing away the snow this morning and shoveling paths from one tent to another, and then a place for Guard mounting.

I went with my assistant Dr. Bradley this morning to the Chapel, and we made a thorough overhauling of the three Indian wounded there. The Doctors who have had them in charge, I don't think were quite as thorough as they might have been. We placed the broken limbs in fixed dressings, and irrigated thoroughly their wounds. We have one colored man in the Hospital Corps here by the name of Fowler. Ask David if he knows him? Seems to me I have seen him before, but can not tell when. He knows all about preparing the antiseptics, and the "1 to 2000 percent solution of Bi Chloride of Mercury."

I can not tell you when I will be relieved. If I was serving in my own department, I should not feel that I am doing some other man's work. I hope that the Surgeon General will take this view of the matter and send me back to my Post, now that the necessity for me coming out here has passed by. It may be that the authorities think that the First Infty who having reached here from Cal. about the time I got here have not had our share of campaigning, and so will keep us as long as they did those who have just returned to their Posts.

Lt. Mallory with whom I have been tenting since my arrival on the 3rd inst started for Omaha today. Now I am all by myself tonight.

With love to you all I remain

Your loving husband,
J.V. Lauderdale

P.S. A beautiful day. The colonel has been out riding in a cutter. Have no news up to this Thursday noon.

J.V.L.

Pine Ridge Agency S.D.
Jan. 29th 1891

Dear Frank,

Yours of the 22nd is before me with a clipping from a Western paper, by Mrs. Dean who was a correspondent of some paper.[92] I am glad to get all the clippings you can send me as they are quite interesting reading. They—the correspondents generally pride on the "agony" in their articles and make out a yarn fully equal to its merits. I see that the 7th cavalry had another mishap on its way home by a collision on the train which destroyed the life of one of its Officers and several of the men.[93] The survivors of the battlefield had to be cut off by the carelessness of the railroad employees.

I do not know how long I will have to remain here. All those Medical Officers who came with me have gone back to their respective Posts, and there is no good reason why I should have to stay. I have not asked to stay, but have requested to be sent back too. Winter campaigning is all very fine, but after the war is over and peace has been restored I would just as soon return to my little family at Ft. Ontario as to be out here in a Sibley tent. I told Joe in a letter today she could drive her ponies out here into camp and take me out for a sleigh ride and I would take her over the historic battle ground of Wounded Knee, or down to the mission or any where else. Our Colonel was out sleigh riding in a cutter with a lady today.

Yes, it is the same Capt. Baldwin that was with us at Ft. Davis who has been here with Gen'l. Miles. He has gone back to Chicago and took with him a party of Indians to meet the people and make such arrangements for their peace and welfare as they require. A telegram from Gen'l Miles today states that the party reached there all right and that the Indians are very happy. This message was communicated to the Sioux families here and I have no doubt that there is great rejoicing in the tepees and homes where they live.

I hope you will cut out any items you may see in the papers on the subject of these Indians and send me. Keep me posted in Geneseo news also. Joe sent me a bundle of papers today, [one] was the Liv. [Livingston County. N.Y.] Republican with Dr. Wadsworth's lengthy address on the Iroquois of your state. It is a very readable article although some what prolix.

This wintery weather causes some sickness in camp for there are always some men that do not know how to keep from taking colds and getting [injured].

With much love to Father and you all I remain,

Your affectionate brother,
J.V. Lauderdale

P.S. I sent you today the only "Trophy" of the recent battle that I have been able to procure.

J.V.L.

Pine Ridge Agency S.D.
Jan. 29th 1891

Dear Joe,

I received the bundle of newspapers containing the Army and Navy Journal, and was glad to pursue it with the other[s] you sent.

We have had a beautiful clear day, but the temperature was too low to make any impression on the snow. There was no wind to speak of, and it has been a beautiful winter day. I wish you could drive this way with your pony team and I would like to ride with you, and we could see something of this country which now is covered with a pure white mantle of snow.

Did you read the editorial comments in the A&N[94] on what Senator Plumb[95] said about making Dr. Ainsworth[96] a Colonel which would put him [in] the Chief Med. Purveyors position, or a place equal in rank. Just my sentiments; Dr. A[insworth] seems to think that because he made some changes in the Pension Office, which Poke did not, or would not make, that forsooth he must be promoted over the heads of a good many better men.

Capt. Pierce who we expected would take hold of the business here when Gen'l. Miles left lies sick in bed. I think he has dyptheria, and don't care much for the position to which he has been assigned. He is a big fat man as you will see by his picture, and would rather live in St. Paul and attend to recruiting for the Army than remain out here among these Indians. He I think would enjoy his Club in the City better than life out here among these Sioux. I wish a good man could be found who is able bodied, and willing to take hold of these Indians and help them on their way to civilization.

I have been examining several more Indians today who are going to enlist as scouts, and some have fine physiques and will make excellent soldiers. They will receive the same wages as those Seminole scouts that we used to have at Ft. Clark, and will be under the command of an Officer of the Army.

Thursday Morning

Last night was the coldest of the season. Water froze in my pail 4 inch[es] thick, and my breath condensed upon my bedclothes. I have a man come and make a fire about 7 o'clock, and when [I] tumble out of my bunk it's warm and comfortable. After a good breakfast of veal chops, scrambled eggs, or soft boiled, oatmeal, potatoes, and coffee. I sit and write you while the Band are [is] playing delightful music for Grand Mounting. I am waiting for Dr. Bradley to go with him and assist him with some of the Indian wounded. I find those felt boots very comfortable these days—the Army riding boots are cold and unfit for this cold weather.

Yours of the 25th rec'd. You may not get this as soon as I intended I was kept so long with Dr. B[radley] dressing wounds at the Chapel that I did not have time to finish this.

Love from

Your loving husband,
J.V.L.

Pine Ridge Agency S.D.
Friday Jan. 30, 1891

Dear Joe,

Your letter of Sunday last came today. You must go to the Ames whist party. Glad that the children are doing well, and that Vance takes part in the play of Sunday School.

First Infantry band playing outside headquarters at Pine Ridge, 1891. Photograph courtesy of the South Dakota State Historical Society.

I cannot tell you when I am coming home. The Medical Director (Bache) left without giving me any satisfaction nor even a word. I had very little satisfaction in talking with him. He was as slow, and uncommunicative as any man I ever met. Cold, and unsympathetic as an iceberg. Having assigned me to duty with this regiment he paid no attention to my wishes to be sent back to my Post, did not even tell me what would be my probable destination, nor when I would be relieved. I got so little satisfaction from him that I addressed a personal note to Dr. Sutherland, requesting that as the emergency which called me here was over that I be sent back to my Post. I have not had time to get an answer from Dr. S[utherland]. I was shown a telegram from Washington this evening inquiring what Doctors are here now. This may have something to do with my request. Of the twenty two or more Army Doctors sent out here there are but four of us left—two here and two at camps near here. If it had not been for Whiskey Gardner playing off sick and returning to Cal. I would I think be at home by this time.

Colonel Dallas Bache ca. 1895, Medical Director, Department of the Platte. Photograph courtesy of the Prints and Photographs Collection, History of Medicine Division, National Library of Medicine, Bethesda, Maryland.

You never told me whether Powell, or rather Mrs. P[owell] painted our storm house? I shall make a fuss about that when I come home if it is not? Did they put in the porcelain bath tub in our bath room? Did they carry the water in a pipe to our laundry? Stopping of those doors between the apartments will be the best thing of all, because I hate to feel that everything I say is heard by my next door neighbor.

You may see Commissioner Morgan's report on Indian Affairs in which he endeavors to show that the issues of beef at this Agency have been full and complete, but those of us on the spot can tell him that it has not been so—that the issue has fallen short at least one or two hundred pounds on every head of cattle, and the consequence has been that the Indians have suffered for food. So large a part of their diet consists of meat that they feel it keenly. If Com. Morgan contends that the issues are full, I may say that he has not looked deep enough into the business and has depended too implicitly upon his agents.[97]

Capt. Pierce who has lately been appointed agent here will have to give place to another. The poor man has had (I found out today) something like an apoplectic shivers before he came here, and has been quite prostrated most of the time. So we will have to get a new one to take his place.

Saturday Morning Jan 31st

The air is sharp this morning, I find my fur-lined coat very comfortable at Inspection, or rather Muster. You must be sure and take Julia to Maude Morgan, I cannot be there if it comes off on the 6th of Feb. I have nothing new to tell you. I feel quite satisfied to think that Capt. Pierce's case becomes clear to us. With love to you all I remain

Your loving husband,

J. V. Lauderdale

Doctors and Hospital Stewards, Pine Ridge, South Dakota, 1891.
Photograph courtesy of the Nebraska State Historical Society.

Pine Ridge Agency S.D.

Dear Joe,

This being the 31st day of Jan. we had our usual muster of the troops. The Soldiers were dressed in their brown padded over coats. I do not remember whether your soldiers have had this overcoat issued them yet. They are intended to take the place of the buffalo over coat which has been worn for many years, but which in the absence of the buffalo have become very scarce, and will be wholly replaced by the brown canvas padded garment.[98]

Lt. Col. Casey[99] mustered the seven companies, and Hospital Corps. The old fellow has as little of the martinet about him as any man who wears soldier clothes, and aside from the men answering to their name when called nothing more is required of them.

I have been examining a number of Indians for Scouts today, and they quite enjoy undergoing the examination. They are as modest as young maidens, and object to being stripped, but submit when they find that it is necessary. We have examined nearly 100, and when we have this number they will be divided in to companies of 25, and will be under command of a judicious officer who will go scouting about the country, and will restore quiet among the restless ones.

We are having very cold weather, I shall expect to see a big cake of ice in my water bucket tomorrow morning. This will try the heat retaining powers for Sibley tents. Our cloth homes are not so dense that we cannot hear our neighbors snore, I can distinctly hear the roar of one sleeper not more than 40 feet from my tent.

The coldest night of the season.

Love to all,
Your loving husband,

J.V. Lauderdale
Pine Ridge Agency S.D.
Feb. 1st, 1891

Dear Joe,

Your good letter of the 28th ult? with one from Frank came today. This has been a very cold day, a wave of unusual severity is passing over us, and as I sat by my stove toasting my feet an orderly brot me your letter. I am glad that you are all so well and that you were able to be at Mrs. Irwin's, and at the Ames whist party. I have money enough for the present, but can not tell just how long I will have to stay, nor how much I will need. I will tell you more of this at another time.

Frank's letter is interesting reading as it is quite a change from what I am having here, dressing wounded Indians who have been riddled with bullets, and men (soldiers) getting sick with colds, and all such grave subjects. Frank's letter is rather interesting reading when she says she thinks she would like to come out here and see the Indians. She has not been among them very much, and they would be a great curiosity to her.

Did I tell you that I enlisted, or rather examined one of those Indians that was with the Forepaugh Circus just last summer? He wore his silver badge a circular plate of silver with "4 Paw" engraved upon it. So you will be interested in the company to which he belongs as you

Blue Whirlwind Woman, who suffered fourteen gunshot and shrapnel wounds at Wounded Knee Creek, 29 December 1890. Photograph by Clarence G. Morledge, courtesy of Rohan Collection, Nebraska State Historical Society.

have seen him. The last Harpers Weekly has a picture of some of our Officers Lt. Strothers,[100] Getty not "Geddy"[101] as the Weekly has it. There is also a picture of Fred Remington, the artist in the same group which is a very correct likeness of the latter as I saw him here.

I was calling at Mr. Cook's this evening, and Miss Shepard (the nurse Bishop Hare sent on to take care of the Indians) asked me if I knew Capt. Mason Jackson, and she said that she took care of him when he was undergoing an operation at Chicago, and that he is not entirely well of it yet.

There are but two Indian wounded remaining in the Chapel and they hold on to life by slender threads. Some of them have gone to get well, and others left to die among their friends. Only the badly wounded came under our care as they were made prisoners, and were obligated to stay for a time, though if they did not care to stay with us they went to their tepees. There was no compulsion about our treatment of any of them.

So Walter has gone to look after his orange groves in the sunny south? Do you see Harpers Monthly. There is a good article by Dudley Wagner on the orange and olive groves of Southern California which I will read as Lt. Winn has kindly loaned me the one for Jan / 91.

One Soldier of this camp lies [low] with acute Cerebritis, took cold because he was not dressed as warm as he should have, and will die. Soldiers are sometimes very careless about exposing themselves to the cold. It is getting late and I will close with love to you all.

Your loving husband,

J.V. Lauderdale

P. S. Coldest night of the season 22 degrees below zero. Frost on my bedding.

Pine Ridge S.D.
Feb. 3rd, 1891

Dear Joe,

I have letters from Father, and Frank. You have no doubt forwarded to Geneseo some letters of mine that were in a complaining spirit, and were not intended for the perusal of Geneseo friends. You must only send such letters as breathe a spirit of perfect acquiescence with my duty as a brave and gallant Officer, who is ready to fight, and bleed, and defend his country, from foes without, and foes within. That is all very fine but you and I know that there is a great deal of favoritism in this same U.S. Army. You will recall a little remark made to me by Col. Henry the day Gen'l. Miles started off, and told H[enry] that he would have to stay till the business was all settled, and then he should return to Fort Robinson a neighboring Post. Now you know that Henry is a thorough going and pain staking Officer, who does his duty thoroughly and if any one should be allowed to return to his Post at an early date it is he.

So according to Father I must "feel quite happy that I am in circumstances to make sacrifices for my country." You will infer that this note is not to go to our Geneseo correspondents, and you may only send those which will put us in a favorable light. I know you will send them any items that they should know, but just rewrite it and not send the originals. I will enclose Father's letter, preserve it.

Frank sends a letter also, and she wants me to send her photographs and tobacco bags, souvenirs, but she is perfectly regardless of the fact that curios cost money and we have enough of such things. I shall have a few photographs to bring with me, but most that I have seen here are very poorly taken and are sold at not less than 50 cents apiece, and I do not care to invest much in them. I regret that I did not bring a hand camera with me, and I should then have some views that it maybe would be of interest to ourselves and friends.

I have read the little clippings from the papers which you sent me, in the two bundles I received from you today. With a good laugh over them, especially the one about Miss G[oodale]. I would not dare to show Miss G[oodale] that little squib. Most all the men think that every good looking girl should hold herself ready to accept the offer of the first man who asks for her hand, but Miss. G[oodale] has marked out for herself a living, a duty of her own choice, and as she can be of good service to the Indian she should be encouraged in her work. Young Eastman is an estimable young man, and if he can win the heart of Miss G[oodale] let him have her. I was in his office the other day and saw a picture of the young lady peering down from his book case.

The answer to my note from S.G. [Surgeon General] about what I expected, and I must wait the movement of things with becoming patience, I get nothing new today. The weather has moderated, and today the snow yielded a little to the rays of the sun.

With a great deal of love to you and the children and Aunt Julia, I remain,

Your loving husband,
J.V. Lauderdale

Pine Ridge Agency S.D.
Wednesday Feb. 4, 91

Dear Joe,

Yours of the 30th ult came to hand today. I am glad that you had a pleasant party at Mrs. Ames'. Was it a dinner party? What part did the dinner play in it? Am glad that you and Julia had the ambulance to yourselves. You must give Julia some good tonic. Not less than six grains of Quinine every day. If I have any of those soft capsules give her some of them. They were in the pigeon hole of my writing desk in the dining room, or the Steward can make some capsules. I believe in some quinine for all such cases, and a good drink of rich milk daily, and then good warm Jaeger flannel from top to toe is very essential to ward off all the chilly currents that will reach one during the early days of spring.

I wish I could get away from this place and return to you, and I would try and make good Marjorie's promise to cure Aunt Julia. I would not have Aunt J[ulia] remain with you if she thinks she would be better in Brooklyn, but hope she may find it as pleasant there as in B [Brooklyn] I do not know who will take J[ulia]'s place of all the sisters. So you have lost your snow, and will have to put the sleigh and bells away for the present.

We have elegant sleighing out here. I wish I had the ponies and sleigh, and would have fine outings with them. I never heard of rats eating lead pipe to get at the water they contain?

I have been busy examining monthly sick reports. During the month of January, we had ninety five cases of sick and wounded on our list, and this did not include any (or not more than one of those) which were sent to us from the battlefield, just such cases as occur in the exposure of soldiers in camp life. You know we have had as many as eight companies during January, and there have been many little accidents, and diseases occurring to man [men] who are not acclimated.

I get no word of any movement of troops. We have not had word on who will be our new Agent, but hope the right man will be found soon.

I have had my tent full of fragrant Sioux this afternoon, whom I have examined as to their fitness for scouts. I added eight more to the list today.

I find the little bundle of papers you send me daily a great help to while away the time, besides keeping me posted in general news.

One of the half breed scouts who can read, read the poem "The Tepee and the Buck" also the little morsel referring to Miss Goodale and was quite amused. He chews gum and smiled, she chewed and grinned showing a beautiful set of teeth. Send us some more.

Love to all from

Your loving husband,
J.V. Lauderdale

Pine Ridge Agency S.D.
Feb. 5, 1891

Dear Joe,

I wish I could have been with you this evening to hear Maude Morgan's harp recital at the Y.M.C.A.'s concert, but this Indian business detains me and all the music I hear is the warbling of certain Indian boys down by their tepees singing, I may suppose to charm their squaws near by. I cannot say that I enjoy the latter very much, but this is all this ridge affords.

This evening the last of our Indian patients left us. There have been but two for a week past, and they required several hours to dress their wounds. One of them had gotten along so that we had some hope of saving her, but her mother came along and the girl saw her and wanted to go to her tepee, and nothing would satisfy but she must go and we will probably hear of her death in a day or two, as she will not have any medical attendance save what her Indian friends may give, and that amounts to nothing. It's strange that these stupid Indians become prejudiced against educated practice, and being without knowledge and patience they take their friends out of the care of those who can care for them and left to themselves to die. It is very unsatisfactory to us, but we are relieved of a great deal of labor, which we were willing to give though there was but little hope.

Your bundle of magazines of Century, Am. Photog, & A&N Journal came today, and I enjoy them very much. I called over at Mrs. Cook's this evening and she loaned a book, and a paper from her library which I find contains some things that interest me. Will you send me by mail Dr. Prime's Autobiography? I think it was in the closet off from the sitting room. Mrs. Cook is a native of Cambridge, granddaughter of old Deacon Sidney Wells of White Meeting house farm, and I would like her to see the book.

Records of a busy life by Dr. Dryer, who was one of old Dr. Tyng's assistants is the book I have from Mrs. C[ook] and contains references to many people and places I am some what familiar with, and therefore entertaining. Dr. D[ryer]'s son was appointed Q.M.U.S.A. because Dr. D[ryer] was a school friend of Lincoln's Secretary Stanton. Influence you know, in politics is a great thing and helps to get soft places in the Army. We do not happen to have any sick, and have to take things as they come and put up with it.

You may send me also a pack of envelopes as I find they go pretty fast at the rate of one letter a day to you.

I will send you a letter I got from Father today. You will see that Mr. Culver paid his note on that Skinner farm mortgage, and we will give him credit for it. The cash book is in the Silver chest. Please place Father's note in the book opposite the account. I think of nothing more to add but love to you all from

Your "darling" husband,
J.V. Lauderdale

Camp Pine Ridge Agency S.D.
Feb. 6th, 1891

Dear Joe,

This day brings something new, and the new item is that a Captain Penny [102] Late Reg. Q.M. of the 6th Infty is to be made Indian Agent in the place of Capt. Pierce, who is unfit for the position on account of illness. The new man belongs to the same Regiment that Capt. Powell does, and the latter must know him. I hope he will fill the bill, and come along as soon as possible and put things at the Agency in order and that will "let us out" sooner.

Today at lunch sat a Mr. Standing who is here from the Carlisle School. He is here to get thirty recruits for the above institution.

Since noon we have had a regular Dakota blizzard. Snow flying through the air in clouds, and the wind flapping the tent ropes in a fitful manner. The snow sifts into my tent in one or two places near the door, but I feel very comfortable, and the cords are firm, and I do not think they will readily yield to the wind unless there should come up a cyclone. The noise of the flapping is disagreeable if you let it attract your attention. I hope that as the sun goes down the wind will lull, as I may not sleep if this noise continues.

9 o'clock P.M. The blizzard blows as hard as ever and the snow is flying along before it in great white sheets of spray. I thot at one time my tent might go, but it holds on very good, and as the pins are frozen into the ground, I do not think it will yield to the blast. It was a stormy night, and I knew I should find Mrs. Cook at home so I went over there (about a stone's throw) to make a call, and pass away a part of the evening in a substantial cottage whose walls unlike my Sibley are not flapping and yielding to the force of the wind.

Miss Shepard the trained nurse was there and the little Indian boy, a survivor of the Wounded Knee fight. Mrs. C[ook] piled up the wood upon the brass andirons, which she told me used to belong to her Grandfather Sidney Wells, and the burning pine sent out a beautiful light, and a genial heat which contrasted with the cold without. We sat and discussed many questions—the Indian, and all other questions growing out of it and the book I had borrowed from Mr. C[ook]'s library to read till I thought the ladies would like a rest, and then I put on my great coat, and floundered thro the snow drifts to my tent and renewed the fire in my little stove, which had got very low in my absence. This is the roughest night I ever spent in a tent. I have not heard either of church bells, and conclude that any gathering of the Indians to worship is not thot of in such dreadful weather. But Dakota blizzards like everything else have an end, and as I sit in the roar and racket of this one and write to you I have a hope that my next letter may be penned under a calmer sky.

Mrs. Cook gave me a book, and Miss Shepard some Christian Unions to read, so I have enough to occupy my mind while the storm rages. Hoping you are well and the children are happy. I remain

Your loving husband,
J.V. Lauderdale

Camp Pine Ridge Agency S.D.
Feb. 6th, 1891

Dear Joe,

Yours of the 1st inst came today and I will proceed this evening to reply to it. Lt. Col. Casey has just left my tent. He likes to come in and get a paper, or a book to read to while away the time which must be to him a great weight, as he has nothing at all to do. Col. Shafter being in command and doing all the commanding, Col. Casey has just to fold his arms and rest on his oars. Col. C[asey] was born in Phila-[Philadelphia] is just about my age, used to live in N.Y. and was of a wealthy family but he was fond of an active life, used to be in the Coal business, a member of Woods gymnasium in 28th St. Ran with a Hose Co. in Amity St., and belonged to the 7th Regiment, till he joined the 5th US Infty. about the breaking out of the war, and since the war has seen a good deal of service on the frontier with Gen'l. Miles. He is now tall and gaunt and suffers a good deal from dyspepsia[103] a slow moving frame much broken in health, and does not like it out here at all, and would like to get back to Benicia [Barracks, California] as soon as he can get ordered there. I feel sorry for any one who cannot find enough to do to keep off ennui.

You better invite those young people to a dinner while Mrs. B. is able to be clothed and in her right mind, and can enjoy it, and while Julia is there to assist you at the dinner.

So you have got back into the buck board again. I expect that you will scarcely get snow enough for more sleighing this winter. They used to tell me that the weather at Oswego during the spring is pretty rough, and you will get enough of it before settled weather can be hoped for.

The Royal family have tried to live off of the government this winter, and have used so much paint on the inside of their house that they must have made Mildred[104] sick, poisoned her with lead. So that she could not eat what little was set before her. When you think that they have been dumping on the paint in some part of their house all winter I am not surprised that they are not all sick. It serves them right if they will make such "pigs of themselves." I am glad that we did not have any painting done in our house this winter, as the smell of it would have made you all sick.

I am glad that Vance is getting more teeth, and hope he will have the strength to pull them through without much suffering to his little system.

We have had a beautiful day with sun shining from a clear sky, and the snow has been melting and running off in little streams across our parade grounds, and so we had to step through little ponds of water here and there to get on dry ground.

Col. Shafter saw by the morning report that I had a larger number of men at sick call than usual, and he called me over to his tent just now to ascertain the why, and wherefore. He is on the alert to know all that happens, the Dr. has to explain everything. He must make life disagreeable to some people. I see about me by his "talking on with so much anxiety" as Bob Russell used to say. With much love to you all.

Your affectionate husband,
J.V. Lauderdale

Pine Ridge Agency S.D.
Feb. 8th, 1891

Dear Joe,

I am happy to say that the ever lasting blizzard which seemed never to be ready to cease has come to a stop since about 8 o'clock this evening, and it has come to such a dead calm that I feel strange when I look at up at my tent, and do not find it heaving and struggling to get away like Prof. Frisbee's balloon just before the ladder is ready to go up. You know all about a Dakota blizzard, and I need not dilate upon that subject, only you will rejoice with me that there is some prospect of getting a good sleep tonight without any feeling that my tent will be prostrated by the wind, and you may rest assured that my tent door will not fly open before I am ready to have it, and if any snow falls, it will not cover my floor with a carpet of white.

Monday Morning.

This will go today but we hear that the roads are obstructed, and snowplow trains have the right of way for a day or two at least.

The day promises beautiful, and the results of the blizzard shows itself in large quantities of snow thrown together in masses, and furrowed out by the wind in miniature ravines and ridges. It is packed as hard as ice cream, and will almost bear your weight. It would afford a good walk for a snow shoe club. Do you hear anything of that club in Oswego this winter? It seems to me that you should have sleighing in O[swego] as we have so much snow here.

One of the Cavalry companies, the 6th that has been camped here with us for a week past will leave today under Lt. Sands,[105] and will take the cars to Rushville and go by rail to Yellow Stone Park where they will remain for a time doing guard and escort duty at the National Park. It seems that one Company of Cavalry is there all the time to keep off intruders—hunters and curio hunters.

Not a word is said about anyone else moving. All the California troops are heartily sick of it here. There is nothing to do, and no changes to make [in the] files, or anything else. The old Col. you know, asked to be sent here it is supposed to distinguish himself and make capital for himself towards a promotion to the next Brigadiership. But the chance of making a reputation have passed, and now he wants to get away as much as anybody.

I have a few recruits for scouts to examine this morning, and I will not write more as they will be here in a few moments, and I will have to take their measurements and the dimensions of their manly chests.

So with love to you all I am as ever.

Your loving husband,
J.V. Lauderdale

Pine Ridge Agency S.D.
Monday Feb. 9th, 1891

Dear Joe,

We live in a country of snow and fierce winds, and the snow has fallen in great quantities and the winds have piled it up and filled the cuts and valleys through which our railroad passes, and the way for our cars loaded with letters and papers has become blocked, and we are necessarily deprived of our communications which become part of our life. The blockade caused by the snow thus destroys for a time, our very existence and we die to each other. The blocking of a mail route to me causes a species of sickness that is like shutting out my supply of fresh air, and I cannot endure it long.

A man came over from Rushville yesterday on horseback, and represented the mail wagon, but brot no mail as there was no mail to bring. It was telegraphed that Lt. Starr[106] would leave there this morning and come in a spring wagon, but he has not put in an appearance and we think he was not able to get through on account of the snow.

Lt. Sands left here with his company of Cavalry for Rushville, but from the indications he will not be able to make more than half the journey by reason of the drifts of snow along the road. So you see that we are quite cut off from the outer world by the expansive fall of snow.

I continue to write you although I am well aware that there is no chance to send this, but from force of habit, I shall jot a few notes.

Today has been Annual issue day of goods to the Indians. I looked on a few moments but it is the same thing we have seen at Ft Bennett, and I have witnessed at Ft. Defiance and the day being pretty cold I did not remain long.

I have just been reading some papers by Capt. Pratt, handed me by Mr. Standing, Capt. P[ratt]'s associate who is here getting recruits for Carlisle, and he believes in breaking up the tribes and diffusing them among the whites as the Negroes (colored people) are, and all other tribes and nations of our country. He does not believe in herding them on reservations living by themselves, and speaking a different language, and following different pursuits.

Tuesday Feb. 10th

There is not much to tell you this morning that is new. No mails through from Rushville, and no communications with the outside world. We hope to get something before the sun sets.

If you and Julia were here, I would invite you to go with me down to the issue rooms and witness them toss out the dry goods and clothing to the Indians who are out in force this beautiful bright day receiving their annuity goods.

With a great deal of love to you all I remain.

> Your loving husband,
> J.V. Lauderdale

> Pine Ridge Agency S.D.
> Tuesday Feb. 10th, 1891

Dear Joe,

It is reported that the snow plow has reached Rushville, and we may get a mail by tomorrow and this may be carried over the road in tomorrow's stage. Lt. Starr who started in an ambulance from Rushville yesterday morning did not get farther than the 9th Cavalry camp (about four miles from here) by five o'clock yesterday, and made his way here this morning. He reported hard packed snow, and harder wheeling.

The issue of Annuity goods has been in progress today. I looked on for a while to see what poor goods they turn over to the Indians for their use as <u>good</u> goods. What crowds of upturned faces some of them painted with little daubs of yellow, and red, and the seam in their hair colored a deep red. The Indians had their wagons, and each blanket load of goods was placed in their wagon, and they drove off to their homes as we have seen them do at Ft. Bennett.

I called over at Mrs. Cook's, and met Miss Goodale who called and I had a little talk with her. She thinks the quality of goods issued this year is very poor.

After Miss G[oodale] had gone, Mr. Standing who had also called remained and Mrs. Cook and I "gave him a private lecture on the subject of sending Carlisle students out here with no possibility of their finding anything to do to earn their living" to all which the little man quietly assented. Mr. S[tanding] is English by birth, but has been at Carlisle for a number of years assisting Capt. Pratt.

Mrs. Cook told me something about Miss Goodale that I did not know. Her Mother and Father do not live together. I could not learn more of the case in the presence of Mr. S[tanding]. I once found out in conversing with Miss. G[oodale] that I may have touched upon a tender subject when talking of her family. Miss G[oodale] goes East in the spring, and expects to be married Tra-la-la-la. She is a lady of good sense, and thoroughly interested in the work of civilizing the Indian. She has a pretty face, and a good figure, but I think I detect a trace of sadness about her, which she tries to overcome by devotion to the duty she has [thrust upon] herself.

This evening the teachers of the boarding school gave a reception as a parting entertainment to those scholars who are about leaving them to go with Mr. S[tanding] to Carlisle. I was invited and went. Calisthenics and music by one of the boys, who plays the melodeon formed the principal part of the performance while I was present.

Your loving husband,
J.V. Lauderdale

P.S. A doubtful prospect of any mail today. Another officer has fallen sick. There is so much poor, flabby humanity in the Army that has no more right to be in it. It comes in civil life, and not through West Point. Could not stand that examination it was brot before it.

J.V.L.

Pine Ridge Agency S.D.
Wednesday February 11th,
1891

Dear Joe,

I shall expect to be disgusted with writing the name of this place before I can get my orders to leave it. I have not felt myself bound down by Army orders as much as I am this winter. There seems to be no way out till the time is up. I cannot do as convicts in State Prison who do well hope to have my days here shorten. The time does drag along so slow, and then to have the mail blocked up by snow on the railroad is disheartening enough.

Yesterday one of the young officers who left his wife and children in California, and has been grieving to go home ever since he came, was out yesterday with his company on mounted drill, returned and had to go to bed. He had an ear ache and neuralgia last night, but today there seems to be brain trouble, and he has been somewhat delirious, although the fever keeps within bounds. It is bad enough to be sick at all while out on a winter campaign, but to have one's mind affected is a very sad state. His mother was insane, and I fear his brain will give way entirely.

This is Ash Wednesday and I see that Mr. Ross[107] an Indian catechist held a service at the little chapel, the first service held since the house was used for the wounded Indians.

The snow has melted some today, and we can see a little more of the earth than has been visible for a week past. I shall hope to get a letter tomorrow but the mail carriers are not very enterprising in this country and they may disappoint us again, though a telegram went round this morning that the road was open both ways and that a snow plow reached Rushville at 11 o'clock today.

I will not write more tonight as I must lay myself away for the night as I may be called up before morning.

> Your loving husband,
> J.V. Lauderdale

P. S. Ten p.m.

I hear the Indian Scouts at their camps blowing "taps" and some of them do it quite as well as the white soldiers.

Thursday Morning

Lt. Winn[108] has just started for Rushville to meet the paymaster and bring him here to pay the waiting assembly.

Lt. Mason[109] does not seem to be any better—perhaps worse—a case of inflammation of the brain from cold and exposure. He had some inflammation of his right ear and probably aggravated it by a long ride in the cold. It does not do to try to make cavalry men of infantry without more experience than these men have had. One man just came to me having been kicked by a horse. Another was run away with, and barely escaped an injury by dropping off his horse.

Love to you all from

> Your loving husband,
> J.V. Lauderdale

> Pine Ridge Agency S.D.
> Thursday Feb. 12, 1891

Dear Joe,

The people of this Ridge are rejoicing today that the mail facilities are once more renewed with the outer world. The telegraph line is open but they do not transmit anything but general news, or military messages. But I am specially delighted that I am in receipt of two letters from you also two bundles of N.Y. & Oswego Times.

I read the letter from Mrs. Smith, and rejoice that Maurice passed safely thro her severe surgical ordeal, and seems to be doing well again. Dr. Villon had assistance from the city?

Glad that the children are quite well again, but what to advise Julia I do not know if she must go home. I do not know who you can ask to come and stay with you, if there is no sister left to take her place. I dislike to think of your being alone a day. Frank I presume would like to come, but do not know as she can leave Father at this time. I regret that I should miss the harp concert, but glad that you and Julia could be present.

It is necessary for all money accounts to be signed by a commissioned officer, and Steward Hill knows that he cannot forward my Hospital Fund account except it is through the Commanding Officer, who ever he may be.

I shall have to go for the C.O. about making his Qrs. so fine and doing little or nothing for our side of the house.

I conclude that you have snow and good sleighing yet? What an elegant transom you must have, about equal to that stained glass in the Steward's quarters. I suppose that Mrs. P[owell] takes patterns after Mrs. Hill in decorating.

I am interested in learning that Vance is trying to say "Pa-pah." You must have him put the emphasis on the last syllable.

Friday Noon

One of our young officers who has been under my care for a few days, developed on Tuesday night after a cold ride in the afternoon, a severe inflammation of his brain. He has been unconscious almost all the time since, and now the vital spark is fast leaving him. Lt. John M. Mason [John S. Jr.] is his name. He is a son-in-law of Gen'l. Ord,[110] and will leave a wife and two children.

I am quite busy and will not write more.

Your loving husband,
J.V. Lauderdale

Pine Ridge Agency S.D.
Feb. 13, 1891

Dear Joe,

Yours of the 5th and 7th came today the latter contained the two checks on N.Y. I enclose in this the check for $100, which you will need for current expenses for the month, and with what I have, $80 and the check for $91.+ I shall have enough to travel with when I get an order to travel.

I do not remember about that S.F. Co. Gas Light dividend $3.47. It may be that I laid it in my cash book (See in Silver chest) on page S.F. Gas Co. and did not acknowledge it. I wish you would determine by looking the matter up, and see if I have given them credit for it. I will just enclose it to you for safe keeping.

In your letter of the 9th you refer to Father's letter, and to that of the S.G. [Surgeon General]. I think myself that the latter effort was an attempt to say something consoling, but I could not expect more from that old piece of ponderosity. He is not much more than a figure head, his mind having long since become somewhat blunted by his habits. Not having had any more than a casual acquaintance, I could not expect he would put himself out very much for me.

After Gardner left I stood next in rank, and of course it naturally developed, upon me the only Major to take Hartsuff's place who returned after a full two months service out here to his Post at Omaha there being no one with the 2nd Infty but a young Asst Surg (Spencer) whom no one would trust, while here Hartsuff had to put him in arrest. It is unfortunate some times to have too much rank.

Dr. Bradley the young doctor who has been my assistant for the past two, or three weeks and whom I have found a well posted and agreeable young surgeon not afraid of duty, left me today to take his old place in Omaha City, as attending surgeon of certain officers and their families in town. He had saved me a great deal of hard labor in dressing wounded Indians, and looking after the sick in the Camp Hospital. His place is taken by Dr. Cabell whose Post is at Niobrara, Nebraska (not far from here). Dr. C[abell] will remain here till this Regiment goes, when he or I will go with them to California. I no doubt would have a good time if I should go to C[alifornia] but I would just as soon go home to you and the children. A telegram came today inquiring how many "traveling rations" there are on hand for this command which, I fain would believe looks as if they will move soon. Dr. Kean [Kane] was over to see us today from his Camp (Col. Henry's) and will come here when this camp breaks up. I told him he could have my place at any moment. I had no intention of remaining any longer than I was obligated to.

Snow, snow, beautiful snow I hope it will keep some of it till I come. Glad you gave it to Powell about the work done on his house—that left window on our side.

Please tell me if the Powells get a new porcelain bath tub. If they do I shall write a private note to someone to find out why we do not have one, as I know Mr. Bennett showed me the approving of it. You remember that P[owell]'s was approved. If they have had it changed to some thing else, and have without one themselves it was so that they could have spent the money on their side some way.

Glad your dinner party was a success. A party for Marjorie and her friends will be the next one in order as she has many now to whom she is indebted. Have it while Aunt Julia is there if she is well enough to assist.

I am glad that Seymore has a foot hold in the old place and is not thrown out. In the mean time he can look about him for something better. It may be that he and Edward will accept an invitation to come and see us for an outing this year.

I have a letter from Frank today also. Hopes I will have to go to California, for it will be such a nice thing to see. Frank wants to know why Miss Goodale don't marry. I sent her a picture of a noble brave, as he lay stiff and frozen upon the battle field, and she thinks he looks like some one she used to know. Says "Have you a Kodak? Why not?" "Ella has had a ladies party" for a wonder. She (Frank) thinks I have been among the Indians so much I would make a good Agent. How would you like that?

Frank informs me that Albert Cheney has a little girl, and that they received my letter acknowledging the receipt of the water colour by way of the dead letter office at Washington, all through the stupidity of the Rutland post master.

Now I will write a letter to M[arjorie] if I have time before the mail leaves. The death of the officer, Lt. Mason has cast a gloom over the Camp as he was a delicate young man and not fit for the duties of a Winter Campaign against Indians in this inhospitable region. He never should have tried. But he did not want to shirk duty, and went beyond his strength.

> With much love, I remain
> Your loving husband,
> J.V. Lauderdale

> Pine Ridge Agency S.D.
> Feb. 14, 1891

Dear Joe,

The paymaster Stanton[111] came today from Rushville, and tomorrow he will pay the troops.

Today an undertaker came from R[ushville] and bore away the casket containing the remains of Lt. M[ason]. Mr. Striking the Presbyterian Missionary conducted a short service at the house of the agent, which the Officers attended. There was a guard of honor, and the band also to make up the procession which accompanied the carriage just to the edge of the camp, and the undertaker took up his route the remainder of the way alone.

The weather has been quite mild and the snow has melted, and it has been quite muddy. The men gave their tents a good cleaning out, and replenished them with a thick carpet of clean hay and hope that they will do better. Some have bad colds.

Must send this unfinished as I have been busy all day.

> Love to all.
> Your affectionate husband,
> J.V. Lauderdale

Pine Ridge Agency S.D.
Feb. 15, 1891

Dear Joe,

I have just sent off a letter that was not completed. I was occupied
last evening and the Pay Master has been paying this morning. Waiting
for one and another occupied me, and I did not attend to my dis-
patches for Ft. Ontario as I am accustomed to do. My Steward sometimes tries my patience. He is a German and wears glasses, and has to
be told so many times to do anything before he gets the idea, and does
not have that "go" in him which characterizes the American. When I
want any thing done in a hurry I hand it to Emil Appel, who compre-
hends an idea at once and does it. The German writes a miserable little
fine script which is scarcely legible, and I would give him a good overhauling if I had time. He is perfectly honest, but so slow. He is a gradu-
ate of Medicine and perhaps thinks it is necessary to be slow and
dignified. While talking of Stewards I wish you would tell Steward Hill
that I read a good letter from him and will reply in a day or two.

It was an interesting sight to see the long lines of Indian Scouts
dressed in their overcoats, and fur caps standing at the pay table taking their pay with the other soldiers. Some of whom have recently been
on the war path. They can have a chance to fight for us instead of
against us, and get better pay for it.

After I had gathered up the funds belonging to the Hospital Corps, I
invited Capts. Armstrong, and Dougherty to go with me to the
Presbyterian Church, but we found after taking our seats that the service was conducted by an Indian Catechist and in Dakota so that Capt
A[Armstrong] and I were not much edified. Capt. D[ougherty] said he
made out some of it as he has lived among the Indians. This evening
there will be a service by Mr. Sterling in English at the same place, and
a circular went round just now inviting all to attend.

I called on Dr. Eastman before lunch for some medicines which he
has in his stock that I needed, and he invited me to a seat and we had
quite a long and friendly chat, and as his affair with Miss G[oodale]
has become public property I congratulated him on his affair. Dr.
E[astman] sat me right on a few points that I have been in error about.

Miss G[oodale] is the daughter of Henry S. Goodale of Northamption, Mass. not Charles as Frank had told me. Miss G[oodale]'s Mother and Father are both literary people and encouraged their children's genius in the same direction. The second daughter is a teacher of painting (I think it is) in the Smith College at Northampton. There is another daughter, younger Rose. Dr. E[astman] told me that Miss. G[oodale]'s father resides in New York City-did not say anything relative to any "separation" of which Mrs. Cook has told me. I would not expect him to refer to subjects that might reflect against his new [friend]. Dr. E[astman] told me that Bishop Hare has been appointed missionary Bishop of Japan and will spend a year there. I remarked that I thought he knew more Dakota than Japanese and would do more good here than there.

8 P.M.

I have just come from the little Presbyterian Chapel (see picture)[112] where Rev. Mr. Standing has been holding forth to a house packed full of soldiers and a few Officers, the kingdom of Christ. Mr. S[tanding] is a plain speaker who tells the truth in a plain fashion without flowers of rhetoric . . . The singing was out of the *Moody and Saintly Sunday Collection* and a lady played upon a Melodeon, a gentleman and a lady assisted the lady who sat at the instrument and Mr. S[tanding] has a good strong voice and formed the leading element in the choir. I have not had a call from Mr. S[tanding] and have thus far learned but little of his work. There has been so much [medical] work and work among the Indians that the subject of religion has not occupied much of our thoughts. The cold blizzard that we have had to weather and fight with have quite diverted the minds of the people from all subjects that naturally receive attention during time of peace.

You relate Buck's breaking through the seat of the sleigh. Hope it was made good as new.

I am puzzled to think what to advise you to do when Julia goes. Do not know of some one you can [secure] to come stay with you. I can not get away from this spot. We can afford to send them a ticket to come and go on. How would you like to return to Brooklyn with J[ulia] and board with the girls till I come, or with Emma? I am sorry that Vance keeps you so wakeful and deprives you of your needed sleep. If you have to be awake with him much it is better to dress in your bath gown or wrapper so that you will not take cold when you get up to wait upon him. I find that I can get up at any time of the night and go out without taking cold because I do not remove all my clothing. I take off only my coat and cardigan jacket and boots. Have not slept with my clothes off since I have been here. All soldiers sleep with their clothes on and only remove them to bathe. I think you add to your cold by getting up so frequently during the night to look after your young man, and if I were you, I would sleep in your bath gown during this cold weather, or something just as warm. Get you a nice warm jacket like the cardigan or some knit goods and then when you rise you will not feel the change so much. You would smother under the weight of the clothing I sleep under.

Try wearing my smoking gown in addition to your other garments but I think something high in the neck would do you more good—something so warm that you would feel warmed without any additional clothing over you.

Tell Marjorie I will reply to her good letter next time. With much love to you and all. I remain,

Your loving husband,
J.V. Lauderdale

Monday Evening Feb. 16 '91

Dear Joe,

I have written my main letter to Marjorie tonight. I received a paper and Dr. Prime's book today from you. I handed the latter over to Mrs. Cook. She will have something to tell me of the people referred to in it later.

These First Infantry people are making a little stir today about returning to Cal and calculate on pulling out on the 24th inst. which is one week from tomorrow. I get no advice as yet what they will do with me. A letter came from Dr. Bache to the Colonel recommending that I go with this command to California, that it will be a holyday [holiday] for me well deserved as I have remained at my Post without kicking. But I am not equipped with a wardrobe to go visiting, and it will take way into March before I get home. Now if I can finish what they have for me to do here by the time these troops leave, I will make a bee line for home, and not extend my observations to the Pacific Coast just at this time, I would prefer to have you with me when I go there. Dr. Cabill, my assistant is very anxious to go and his Post, Niobrara, is near here and he has sent for his clothes, and I do not care to stand in the way of his going. I have greater interests in the East than in the West. But do not cease your papers or letters till I advise you.

With a great deal of love I remain,

Your loving husband,
J.V. Lauderdale

P.S. I wrote the Steward a short letter today. I do not think of anything to tell him to have done in the line of repairs at the hospital.

Pine Ridge Agency S.D.
Feb. 17, 1891

Dear Joe,

Yours of the 12th inst. came duly to hand today. You had not received a letter from me in three days—and all on account of the blizzard which we had a week ago last Sunday. This will account for the non-appearance of my letters which have been regularly deposited in this office every day since I reached here the 3rd of Jan. last—45 letters all told, good bad and indifferent that I have sent you to keep you in good heart during my absences. Today the men who have been mounted turned in their saddles and tomorrow they will turn over their horses to their owner. It has been another busy day in this Post. After sick call I went to the hospital and waited for the Steward to come. In the mean time I looked after the clothing of one of the patients we are going to send to Ft. Robinson on the first pleasant day.

It is our object now to reduce the sick list to the lowest number so that when the present garrison go there will be as few as possible remaining. My assistant Dr. Cabell is making his preparations to go to California. He has a brother at San Francisco he wishes to see. I shall be alone for a day or two.

Hospital Tents, Pine Ridge, South Dakota, 1891. Photograph by Clarence G. Morledge, courtesy of Rohan Collection Nebraska State Historical Society.

The closing of this business is so slow that I am frequently at the point of resigning. My patience often fails me and I am just on the verge of writing a complaining letter to the Adjt. Gen'l. If there were not so many just like myself who can make just the same complaint. I would send forth lamentations every day, now that this regiment is making preparations to go, about the day this reaches you. I will have hope that I may get my orders to go too. But as I have said do not stop writing or sending me the papers till I say so, for to be in this uncomfortable place without letters and papers is horrid. Col. Casey and I have frequent chats these days together and we try to console one another on the situation. The Col. is a widower his wife was Miss Thorton of N.Y. or up the

Hudson somewhere. He has four daughters, young ladies at home in Benicia who are anxious to see their father at home again.

I am glad that Julia is getting better of her cold.

You must hold the reins on Buck as much as on the ponies, he gets careless. There is no need of those animals running out [where] there is no grass, and if they find nothing to eat they will likely eat up each other.

I read Dr. Talmadge's sermon on Snowflakes and it is quite a well written document. I see that Mr. Bacon has a new book which I must have, "Bibles within the Bible." It is out yet?

With a great deal of love to you, and indignation for the administration that keeps me out here. I remain,

Yours lovingly,

J.V. Lauderdale

P.S. Don't send this to G

Pine Ridge Agency S.D.

Feb. 18th, 1891

Dear Joe,

Col. Casey just passed out of my tent. He said he was in the chapel this afternoon, and while looking at the altaer read an inscription on a brass plate on the lectern or reading desk; which stated that this desk used to stand in the chapel of a church (Episcopal) in 4th Avenue N.Y. when Dr. Francis S. Hawks was its pastor. The Col. said it carried him back to the days of his youth, when he used to attend that church and listen to the famous preacher above named. He, Dr. H[awks], was an orator of great fame in his day. I remember him.

This has been a beautiful day mild and melting as to the snow. I thought it a good day to send off Davis[113] the last of the Wounded Knee patients. His leg was amputated on the 24th of Jan. and he was so far recovered that he could be sent to Rushville and Ft. Robinson without danger. I spent some time lining the ambulance with blankets and arranging the mattress, and pillows, and putting in hot bricks so as to make him comfortable, and we sent him off in good shape.

I find I must get rid of my cases on hand before I can close up this Field Hospital to the satisfaction of Med. Director Bache, if I ever expect to get away from this place myself. Bache telegraphed me tonight that it will be necessary to keep the Hospital open after the First Infty. go on the 26th. (You see they have added two days more to the time they intend to keep the First here.) I replied by telegram that I had sent off my worst cases, and had but one case that was serious that all the rest were walking patients.

Bache seems to be possessed of a almost fiendish spirit in trying to find some excuse for keeping me here. I do not know what makes him act so, unless he is trying to make capital for himself in searching after the position of Surgeon General, and desires to show his zeal in the cause.

My young friend, and assistant Dr. Cabell was very much disappointed today to learn that Dr. Kendall[114] from Ft. D.A. Russell has been ordered to accompany this Regiment to California. He has been busy packing his pannier today for the trip, and anticipated a great amount of pleasure in going, but his hopes are blasted. The First were cast down when they heard it because they don't like Kendall.

The First Infty are getting their fill of this service and the old man will not ask for any more of it, it is so unprofitable in results such as military renown.

The Indian who killed Lt. Casey was brot into camp today, but the Col. sent him under escort to Ft. Mead at once.[115] I sent him some lunch, or requested the Col. to have some sent to him while he rested in the ward tent.

No letter or paper from you today to Your loving husband

J.V. Lauderdale

Don't send this to Geneseo

Pine Ridge Agency S.D.
Thursday Feb. 19th, 1891

Dear Joe,

I have your bundle of papers including the Army and Navy Journal to pursue this evening. I have been quite busy today at the Hospital, signing my name to enlistment papers for the Indian Scouts which have appeared before me during the past month and more. I have signed my name today <u>two hundred and eighty-four</u> times—just double the number of scouts that we have passed as each scout has his papers made out in duplicate. I may be able some day to give you a list of these Dakota gentlemen who have sworn alliance to defend their country against all foes without, and especially all dissensions within her boarders.

I have a letter from Bache today directing me to turn the property of this Field Hospital (which I have told you already is not in "a field" tent, but in one of the agency buildings), or at least as much of it as he wished over to Ass't Surgeon Kean now serving with Colonel Henry's command near here as soon as this First Infantry leaves. To send the balance of it to Fort Robinson and Fort Douglass which will leave me to close up the establishment in due form, if there are no cases that require Hospital treatment at that time.

He does not tell me what he will do with me when I close up the Field Hospital probably leaves that fact to be decided at a later day. I sincerely hope that we will not have any accessions to our sicklist, but that all who are now in Hospital will be able to move with the command when it takes its departure. There is but one now that there is any doubt about his going.

I see by the A&N that Gen'l Miles has very decided convictions relative to the responsibility of Col. Forsyth for the Wounded Knee affair, and I think Gen'l M[iles] is quite right about the matter. The Secretary of War who probably knows as much about war and Indians as Vance, may sit in his office and make up his mind about it, and write something favorable to the old Colonel, but it all goes for naught with us who know something of the situation of things out here.[116]

It has been snowing finely today, and I hope the storm has extended as far East as Oswego so that you will have more rides over the pure white streets, before you have to take to the buck board and muddy streets. I see it is getting late and I will not say more tonight. I congratulate myself in sending off one of my patients to Ft. Robinson before the change in the weather.

With much love to you all

I remain Your loving husband,
J.V. Lauderdale

P.S. Better not send this to Geneseo

J.V.L.

Pine Ridge Agency S.D.
Feb. 20th, 1891

Dear Joe,

Your long two sheet letter of the 13th inst came today, and I was glad to get it. The Harpers Weekly came also. Let me say here not to send any more Harpers, nor Centuries, but send the daily papers as usual for the present.

Oh the blizzard interrupted correspondence quite some—a little thing we often have to endure in the west, in winter time.

Glad that you remembered yourself on your birthday, and that Julia did not forget it. If I had been home I would have made the presentation in person.

I think those inside blinds are just as unnecessary as anything else those people do. I do give them credit for shutting up the partition doors which is about the best of all. The inside blinds are to take the place of curtains, which they do not have money to buy. They are pigs and pigs only. I was just telling Col. Casey about their performance and he says I ought to make a "fuss" about it. It is the reputation of the P[owell] family where ever they have served to be selfish and sneak around and get all they can.

The first time I had an inspection of old hospital property P[owell] was there, and certain old door mats that were ordered to be destroyed he, P[owell] had sent up to his house for his own use. I will see next time that he does not get a thing.

The sickness of this command has been due to the fact that the men came on here from the mild climate of California to endure the rigors of winter and were not acclimated. They did not, some of them, dress warm enough. I went around one day and saw that every man wore two woolen shirts at least, we have so many men coughing.

These troops were sent out to fight Indians because their Colonel asked for the detail as he wanted to make a little capital—perhaps get the next Brigadiership. He has got enough of it already, and wants to get back as soon as he can to Cal. I heard a soldier say today that he would rather be hung in California, than die a natural death at Pine Ridge, he hates the place so. Just this moment I heard the Colonel in the next tent, you ought to see him riding around in a cutter every morning inspecting the Post. How is that for an Inspecting Officer?

Young Man Afraid of His Horses, and another Chief returned today. I think Mr. Cook has also returned, but I have been so busy I did not get over to see him. The Chiefs shook hands with me very cordially, associating with the President has not made them vain and proud.[117]

Troops have been needed here to settle up all the troubles, and will gradually get off and leave things to the Indian Scouts who will be responsible for good order on the reservation.

Glad that Julia and the children and you are all so well give them my love.

I am ordered to turn over my property and will close this Hospital just as soon as the sick are well enough to get away. Continue to write to

Your loving husband,
J.V. Lauderdale

Pine Ridge Agency S.D.
Sunday P.M. Feb. 22nd, 1891

Dear Joe,

When I left Mr. Cook's last evening he told me that Mr. Cleveland[118] would conduct a service in English, so I told the Officers of this mess that such would be the fact. No one however put in an appearance at the Chapel but Dr. Cabell and I. It was thought that it would be best to have the service in Dakota and Mr. Cleveland came prepared to speak in that language, so Mr. Cook had to apologize—I suppose to us. They concluded that the scholars of the school would not be there, only the adults—Indian men and women about the Agency. But while they were singing the first hymn the whole school came marching in the girls taking

Seven of the Lakota leaders in Washington, February 1891. Photograph courtesy of the Nebraska State Historical Society.

seats on one side, and the boys on the other. So that with the adults and the school the house was pretty well filled. The usual morning service of the Episcopal Church was read with singing and responses in which they all joined their deep base voices.

Miss Goodale and Dr. Eastman came a little late and took a seat behind Dr. C[abell] and myself. The service was not very edifying to Dr. Cabell and me, but I was surprised at the fluency of Priest Cleveland who must be well up in Dakota if I could judge him by the ease with which he extemporized in the language of the natives. When the plate for the offering passed around Mr. Cook recited the usual tenets of Scripture, alternately in Dakota, and English, as it would be rather rude to take our silver, even in these days of freecoinage agitation, without some assurances. Sunday school was announced for two o'clock, but I think I will attend the Presbyterian Chapel this evening.

As I passed out I tried to get Miss G[oodale]'s eye but she did not give me a chance. The Doctor saluted me, and is really the most agreeable of the two. I don't know whether she is embarrassed—something queer about her—[the frivolous] are very much inclined to be queer. As I passed out of the little chapel, I could not but recall its appearance when I first entered it a few weeks since, when the floor was covered with the torn and wounded Indians gathered from the battle field lying upon their beds of straw and some crying out with pain, and here and there one passing over the river "to the happy hunting grounds" beyond.

Interior of the Episcopal Church after all of the wounded Lakota were removed. Photograph by Clarence G. Morledge, courtesy of Rohan Collection, Nebraska State Historical Society.

Have just been examining another Indian who desires to enlist as a Scout. I suppose it must be considered as a work of "necessity as well as mercy" for the poor fellow needs his rations and pay.

Your good letter came (that of the 17th). You had been to lunch at the Churchills. It was probably a Miss. Haskins you met. Her father was with us at Ft. Hamilton. Mr. Bacon and his wife are quite success- ful in getting up sociables and concerts. Poor little [tike] to have to leave its mate—and it needs a great deal of attention too.

I hope you will give Vance an airing every fair day so as to keep him well.

Going to California with troops would not entitle me to any mileage. Coming from there to the East would. As I have told you I do not care much for the trip as my wardrobe is not such as I need to go there. As soon as I can close this Field Hospital, and dispose of the property, I shall be ready for the order sending me home. I may have some sick men to look after which will keep me. You cannot hurry the sick, the only thing to do is get the regiment off and there may not be any more to treat.

Mrs. Mason gets $3000 from her husband's life ins. policy.

I wrote to the Steward to prepare such estimates for repairs to the Hospital as he finds necessary and send to me for signature. You can tell him so if he did not understand me. He may include the falling stove pipe and any other thing that is out of order.

I attended the Presbyterian Chapel this evening and listen[ed] to Mr. Standing who made an appeal to the audience, which consisted mostly of soldiers, to step over the line as to be on the right side. He illustrated his idea by a drawing which he had made upon a black board just at the back of the platform. They sang some soul stirring hymns such as "Over the Line" and "I Am Satisfied" from out of the *Moody and Sunday Collection.*

Just now a soldier of the Guard sent for me to come and see him, the weather is not favorable for health and some of our soldiers the German and Swiss don't seem to know enough to enjoy good health, and they are frequently getting out of order in some way. I am hoping to get this whole command off without leaving any sick behind, but I may be mistaken in my plans and have to keep my hospital open longer than I care to. You remember what a time I had in closing my hospital in Atlanta. The best way to close a hospital is to move the command, for there is bound to be somebody who will get sick just as long as soldiers continue to remain about in the vicinity.

With my best love to you all

I remain,

Your loving husband,
J.V. Lauderdale

Pine Ridge Agency S.D.
Feb. 23rd, 1891

Dear Joe,

I have just laid the Oswego, and N.Y. Times down after pursuing it for the evening's feast of news. I do not know what I should do without the Times to keep myself posted in Eastern news. The Western press does not have any news for me.

I have been occupied today with paper work and other business pertaining to the closing up of this Hospital. But while I am trying to wind up the concern, the soldiers are falling sick one by one with colds, fever and pneumonia which looks like keeping the mill grinding longer than we care for. The weather is not favorable for health, and the recent payday has given the men plenty of money, and they have indulged their appetites for pies and cakes to the exclusion of more substantial food, and in consequence they fall sick.

Later—I was out on the line today noon to see about sixty of our soldiers start off in wagons for Rushville. It is that portion of the California column who at their own request wish to be transferred to Regiments serving in this region. So their sweethearts will not see them marching down the Pacific slope very soon. They go to new fields and pastures green.

The men have been too much crowded in their tents and the departure of the above will give those who remain more room. I went around among the tents this evening to see how the men made up their beds, and found that many of them do not know how to make up their beds at night, for many of them place their ponchos, or the impervious covering, not next to the ground, but as like as any way just beneath them, or perhaps over them so that they retain all the emanations of moisture from the ground instead of keeping it out of their clothing.

I was introduced to Standing Elk, one of the Dakotas who recently returned from the East, and he was telling us by gestures and in imperfect English of some things he saw. S.E. [Standing Elk] is a rather portly figure carries a silver headed cane and something of the "bon homme" in his manner. He told of the lofty buildings that rise towards the sky and of his visit to the theater, and as he caught hold of the skirt

The Sioux Delegation to Washington, February 1891. Photograph courtesy of the Nebraska State Historical Society.

of his coat with each hand and held them out on each side and lifted up first one leg then the other in line with his skirts. It was plain to be seen what had impressed him most while there. He is as jolly, and as full of good nature as any man of his tribe.

I met Mr. Sword[119] another Dakota gentleman the Chief of Indian Police, and he is as courtly in bearing and as dignified, as some of those Mexican gentleman we used to see down in Mexico, and I could not but be reminded of them save for those barbaric perforations in the upper rims of his ears.

Every body in camp is counting the hours to the time of their departure—some of their heavy stuff went today. Thursday morning at six o'clock I will take my last meal with the First Infty. We've had a mild day and just warm enough to melt the snow.

With a great deal of love to you all

I remain Your loving husband,
J.V. Lauderdale

Pine Ridge Agency S.D.
Tuesday Feb. 24, 1891

Dear Joe,

I had a little leisure this afternoon and stepped in to Capt. Pierce's office to see how he was getting on. The Captain has been here three weeks since his successor was appointed, and Captain Penny does not yet materialize.

I found the Captain taking down the narrative of Mrs. Few Tails who had such a narrow escape in the attack upon her party by the cowboys. The Captain intends sending her report of the affair to Head Qrs. so that the case may be properly represented to the authorities who will bring the offenders to justice.[120]

Yesterday I was getting the names of some of the Indians wounded, and called upon one Lee [Lea][121] who is employed by Govt to take the names of all the Indians for which he receives pay at the rate of $20 a day. Now I will tell you how this man earns his money. Col. Casey tells me that he sits in his window and spends a good part of his time playing checkers to while away the time that he should be occupied enumerating the Indians. This same Lee [Lea] is the Editor of a paper in Nebraska and declares that the Indians will break out again in the spring. He commands a standing Army at this point to preserve order among the Indians. I think that the reason he takes this position is that he thinks it would be a good thing for the country, and for his newspaper to have troops kept at this Agency as it is a good thing for the country as it brings in money.

He probably feels as one of the citizens I saw today selling pies and things to the soldiers. He said "Boys I feel sorry that you are going off so soon, as I like to have you here. I shall try and meet you on Thursday noon while you are on your way to Rushville and shall have something to sell you then."

Everyone has some axe to grind, some benefit to derive from the situation.

A telegram came this afternoon to have my assistant Dr. Cabell remain here. He was expecting to go along with the troops on Thursday to Ft. Niobrara, his proper station. I think the change is in view of the fact that we have a few sick who will not be able to go with the command when they start on Thursday to return to California.

Dr. Kendall who goes with the First Infty was expected today but was probably detained by the snow blockade on the road west of Rushville. The Colonel says "There will be h—l to pay" if they are detained by snow when they get started.

Well we hope that one order may come someday for the subscriber to go East in which I dare say his wife and babies would join him in wishing that such would be the case.

Your loving husband,
J.V. Lauderdale

P.S. Reports say R.R. blocked to East of us, so letters will be delayed a day or two.

J.V.L.

Agent's Residence
Camp Pine Ridge S.D.
Feb. 26th 1891

Dear Joe,

Your letters of the 19th, and last Saturday came today. There was a little delay owing to a small sized blizzard so that I get two on the same day. You tell me of your nice lunch at the Churchills and those you met there. I think a great deal of Major Haskins, and any attentions you may show his daughter will come back to us. It would be a nice place for Julia to call and see her at Gov. Island.

I am afraid them Powells will get themselves into trouble with you and old Mrs K. after them and the Q.M. down at N.Y. I suppose you have had a day of rejoicing over that new door knob and latch. I am greatly interested in hearing how you came to write the Q.M. I have had it in my mind when I got home to write a personal note to Inspector Hughes whom we know very well, and ask him if we cannot have some of the good things that are going. I think I should be reimbursed in some way for the money I paid for paint put on our quarters last summer, $4.69 I think it was. Powell could just as well as not have made me even for that, but he declared it could not be done.

Marjorie must have eaten something the day before that did not agree with her? It may have been too much candy. I have a letter from Frank and she says she has offered to go and stay with you, but I guess you will think it not worth the while if I get home about the 5th of next month as I hope to do. I say "hope" but with the sick on hand I cannot set any day.

We rose an hour earlier this morning than usual, so as to be able to take an early breakfast with our companions of the First Infty. and to see them strike tents and get under weight to the R.R. All those Sibley tents which have formed such a conspicuous feature on the slope fronting the little Episcopal Church have disappeared from view. The work of removing them began by digging up the tent pins which had become frozen in the ground, and then taking down the central stove and the supporting pole and its bipod, you remember how a Sibley is put up. Each squad of men worked away at their own tent and soon the canvas was rolled up into a heap like Prof. Frisbee's balloon and laid in wagons. The men rolled their blankets into little bundles, and when the wagons came along they took the hay that they had used for their beds and put it into the wagons and with their baggage, they had comfortable seats for themselves. When they had stretched out and got in motion they formed a long line of wagons filled with brown coats and fur caps.

Cols. Shafer and Casey and the Officers of the Staff rode their horses, an ambulance or spring wagon took the rest of the Officers. Dr. Kimball [Kendall] the Surgeon rode on the Red Cross ambulance. We heard they reached Rushville alright. The old Colonel who has varicose veins had a horse and cutter to ride in, and the Officers of the 9th Cavalry who met them on the road made a good deal of fun over the military appearance of this Regiment as they appeared on the march.

I have been busy getting my paper work completed preparing to turn over my property. With the departure of our mess I sit at the neat table of Mrs. Finlay[122] where I took my meals when I first arrived here.

With a great deal of love and kisses for you and the children. I remain,

Your loving husband,
J.V. Lauderdale

Finlay's Trading Post and Hotel, shown here in July 1891, where Lauderdale took his meals after the First Infantry returned to California. Photo courtesy of the National Anthropological Collections, Smithsonian Institution.

Agent's Residence
Pine Ridge Agency S.D.
Thursday 9 a.m. Feb. 26, '91

Dear Joe,

I have just been on the old Camp Ground seeing the First Infty. strike their tents, and gathering up their effects and tumble everything themselves included, into wagons and start for Rushville. They have no sooner got under way when the scouts from the camp nearby advanced on the grounds and will occupy it for the time being.

But best of all a telegram from Washington relieving me from duty with the First Infty, and orders me to my station. As I have some business to do in closing up and turning over the property to the Q.M. for shipment I shall be busy from this time till Monday noon when I shall leave the Ridge, and make my way as rapidly as I can to Ft. Ontario.

I have not time to say more this morning, but will send other notes till I leave altogether. You know what to expect, and I know of nothing that will interrupt the above plan.

> Your loving husband,
> J.V. Lauderdale

> Agency Residence
> Pine Ridge Agency S.D.
> Feb. 27th, 1891

Dear Joe,

I received two papers from you today one containing the program of the old folks concert at Mr. Bacon's Church. The other an Army & Navy in which "Two Strikes" records the blizzard at Rosebud Agency. It was very like the one we had here.

In my letter today I said that my business might detain me longer than Monday next, as I could find no one of my Juniors here or here abouts to take the Hospital property, and funds off my hands. Dr. Cabell did not care for it, and Dr. Kean said he did not need it as he had hospital accommodations for all of his patients at his camp six miles distant. Col. Henry who is really the C.O. here but who does not much care for the position came up this morning, and he directed Dr. Cabell to take charge of the property forth with and let me be off. I had already telegraphed to the Med Director Bache for him to tell me what to do with the property, and about noon I was handed a message that Dr. Kean would have to come forward and take charge of the Camp Hospital, and the property belonging to it whether he wished to do so or not, and Dr. Cabell would remain to assist him. That settled the question for me and now I have Steward Appel making out all the property papers and tomorrow I shall turn over everything to Dr. K[ean].

I am sorry to say that acting Steward Appel is in arrest. He is the young man that was so attentive to one of the young ladies at Ft. Davis, the Comsy. Sergt's [commissary sergeant's] daughter. There was a quantity of coffee and bacon and other things—savings which he was

Hospital Steward Emil Appel (first row sitting on right) at Fort Davis, Texas, ca. 1896. Photograph courtesy of the Nebraska State Historical Society

told to sell, but instead of turning over the money to me, he gave some of it away to those of the Corps that he had made his friends and others. Two colored men did not get anything and one of them "squealed" on him and the squeal came to my ears. He took advantage of the hurrying times to do a little stealing for himself. He has made up a story of the affair which he has submitted to me but it don't clear up the case for himself, and I cannot ask to have the charges withdrawn as he does not account for everything.

He is my only penman and I have to use him to do all my writing. It is very annoying to me to make these discoveries just at this time, but he, Appel has caught the disease which has been so prevalent at this Agency that of appropriating what does not belong to the individual.

The weather is very cold no wind but the mercury will run lower than any night this winter. I am glad that I am in a house instead of a Sibley tent although I have suffered scarcely any from the cold during this campaign.

With a great deal of love to all, and expecting to see you some day next week. I remain,

> Your loving husband,
> J.V. Lauderdale

P.S. Col. Henry says he will send me down to Rushville on Monday the 2nd and I shall leave there the same evening.

> J.V.L.

> Agency Residence
> Camp Pine Ridge S.D.
> Sat. Feb. 28th 1891

Dear Joe,

I completed the work of turning over my property at the Field Hospital today, and this evening I signed the last paper transferring the property to Dr. Kean who with his assistant, Dr. Cabell will take care of the sick now there, or that may be taken in during the stay of regulars or Scouts.

I received the Times today as usual and have just laid it down. I pursued the Oswego Times also and read Mr. Swift's last Sunday discourse.

I expect that tomorrow will prove to be a long day, but I shall get my dry goods in shape, take a bath and remove some of the Pine Ridge dust from my feet, and the next day take up my line of march for the East.

This will be the last line you will get from this Ridge. As I shall probably travel as fast as the mail, and it will not be worth while to send a telegram till I get some ways East of the Mississippi.

> Sunday morning. [March 1, 1891]

Have had my breakfast, and will walk over to the little Chapel with Dr. Cabell and listen to an English service today. I am not enough of a

Dakota scholar to listen attentively to the word when it is dispensed in the above tongue from the lips of the most gifted teachers.

Later;

Have just come from the little Chapel where I found Rev's Cleveland, and Cook in their places with Mr. Ross as a catechist robed and in their right mind. The services were in the language which I am most familiar with, and with plenty of Hymns and Prayerbooks I had no difficulty in following it.

The children of the boarding school, girls were in their places when we got there, the boys came in later. Mr. C[ook] delivered a fairly interesting Lenten homily and we were quite edified.

There was an addition to our snow last night and the sleighing must be very fine. I wish I had a sleigh to take me over to Rushville tomorrow.

I learned that Capt. Penny the new agent is coming tomorrow with his family. He has the wagon that Col. Henry was to give me so I shall have to take some kind of public conveyance.

I will not add more as I expect to follow this letter on the morrow. Shall telegraph when I can calculate on meeting the ambulance at the Oswego station.

> Love to all,
> Your loving husband,
> J.V. Lauderdale

> Cody, Neb. March 3, 1891
> Palace Car, Neb. R.R. en route
> to the East Snow Bound.

Dear Frank,

Yesterday, Monday at 2 o'clock, I left Pine Ridge in a two horse buggy—the stage which carries our mails to and from Rushville and rode along very comfortably with the wind at our backs. At a distance of seven miles from the Agency I passed Col. Henry's camp of four companies below in a little valley a stone's throw from the road. Two of his "buffalo soldiers" as the Indians call the colored troops were standing by the road side to hand us some letters to be mailed. As we approached the high lands a few miles from R[ushville] the wind increased, and the fine snow that our wheels threw up followed us and was blown up in front of us and came back into our faces and covered our coats with a white mantle. It was not warm enough to melt and we did not suffer. The wind blew sharp and tried to penetrate under our robes but it did not chill. One of the horses old and pretty well played out began to lag behind the other, and after a few miles of tugging had to be dragged along by the other horse. If we were to be shut down in such a storm and have to walk in we were of all men most miserable, but our driver knew a ranch man along the road and called to see him and asked for the loan of one of his horses which he kindly loaned, and putting in a good pack horse, we rolled through the snow and storm and came into Rushville just after dark.

Arriving at the station I opened the trunk and packed my robe and purchased my ticket for Syracuse—could do no better. After a study of routes I decided on the Grand Trunk out of Chicago. I put up at the N.W. Hotel and got supper, and then went to call on Capt. Penny the new Ind. Agent who is waiting to go to his post as soon as the weather is favorable (He will go today as it is perfectly lovely). I found the Captain a gentleman of good appearance—not a crank a person of good sense, and one who in my opinion capable of conducting the affairs of an agency or any other business. I would think him a good man to superintend almost any kind of business. I did not think much of Capt. Pierce— he was a heavy lump of humanity rather too heavy to manage the affairs of an Indian Agency. I did not see Mrs. P[enny] although she was along and will be with her husband which is the right thing for an agent. Old man Pierce was a bachelor, and of course would have around him a different set and would not be above suspicion of having a set about him that would not minister to his reputation.

I slept until about midnight, and then took the train and reached here about five o'clock this morning where we have remained snow bound— at this moment about six hours. How much longer we must stay here cannot be determined by the people here. We have a comfortable car, a station eating house close by and to while away the time I have been reading over old letters, some from you and am now penning one to you. It is better to be here than dwelling in a tent, but when one would like to be nearing the Missouri River it is not pleasant to be snow bound fifty miles from the place of starting. I hope to get to Oswego before Saturday night. With much love to you and Father and the families.

I remain your affectionate brother,
J. V. Lauderdale

P.S. Were detained about twelve hours when a snow plow came from the East opening up our road.

Chapter Three

After Pine Ridge

Dr. Lauderdale departed Pine Ridge on 2 March 1891, arriving home on 5 March. With the exception of his being snowbound for twelve hours, his journey was uneventful. The remainder of his tour at Fort Ontario proved equally uneventful, his duties those of an army post doctor. Excluding the ongoing disharmony with their neighbors, Dr. and Mrs. Powell, the Lauderdales enjoyed their post and home.

The doctor relished his family life and shared the various cultural activities of New York with them. He joined the Fortnightly Club of Oswego, as mentioned in his letter of 16 January 1891. On 2 June 1891 he presented a paper on the Dakota Indians to the assembled members. Unfortunately, the text of the paper has not been preserved. Lauderdale, Joe, and the children were active in local church and civic functions. His medical duties at the fort allowed ample time to enjoy the children. He took special pleasure in Marjorie's singing ability, and wrote his praise for her to Frank regularly. As always he remained mindful of the news of the day. Like most citizens, the economic situation in the 1890s troubled him.

The depression of 1893 caused profits at George Pullman's railcar factory in Chicago to diminish. Pullman's workers lived in company-owned housing, shopped at company-owned stores, and their children attended company schools. The company also controlled the water and gas systems. Sinking profits induced Pullman to reduce the pay of his workers 25 to 40 percent, while holding rent and other prices unchanged. In May of 1894 the workers, most of whom were members of the American Railway Union, staged a strike.[1]

Led by Eugene V. Debs, the strike immobilized rail traffic in and out of Chicago.[2]

Under the pretext of ensuring delivery of the mails, the federal Government intervened. Seeking to crush the union and humble Mr. Debs, President Cleveland ordered the army to Chicago to reopen the rail lines, mob action had destroyed some seventy rail cars. The strikers, while at times violent, showed no aggression toward the army.

In July of 1894 Lauderdale accompanied troops from Fort Ontario to Chicago. In a 10 July 1894, journal entry from the Lake Front in Chicago, Lauderdale blamed Pullman's "avarice" for the strike. While in Chicago, he renewed acquaintances with some of the officers he had served with at Pine Ridge. Among the officers mentioned in his journal was Dr. Ives, and General Miles commanded the entire force.

On the 16th of July a Hotchkiss gun exploded, apparently by accident. The explosion killed four soldiers and wounded seven others, and two of the wounded suffered severe burns. Dr. Lauderdale treated some of the wounded. The railroad duty lasted but a short time and he was soon back home at Fort Ontario for the remainder of his tour.

Lauderdale's last tour before retirement sent the family westward again.

The Lauderdales reported to Fort Omaha, Nebraska, in January 1895. At Fort Omaha he found more old friends from the Pine Ridge campaign: General Brooke still commanded the Department of the Platte, which was headquartered at the fort, and Lauderdale's immediate supervisor, the post medical director, was his old nemesis, Colonel Dallas Bache. The animosity between the two, so evident at Pine Ridge, was absent from Lauderdale's writings at Fort Omaha.

Colonel Bache had married Colonel James Forsyth's daughter in November of 1891,[3] and the couple paid a social call on the Lauderdales. By April of 1895, Mrs. Bache was pregnant. Lauderdale made a journal entry on 4 May 1895, "Dr. B[aches]'s wife is younger than some of her children, and I was a little confused till I heard Miss B[ache] [Bache's daughter] call the Dr. 'PaPa'." A tentative friendship developed between the Lauderdales and the Baches, and the two families exchanged frequent social calls. Social calls among the other officers, similarly, increased at Fort Omaha.

The city afforded many opportunities for concerts, recitals, lectures, church plays, opera, and the theater. Trips to nearby parks, boating, and just walking brought the family together often. Marjorie was in the cast of many recitals and church plays, and her performances brought much pride to her father. The family loved to ride the street cars that crisscrossed the city, and they frequented the city's amusement park, "Manowah," just across the Missouri River in Iowa. Attendance at one of Buffalo Bill's Wild West shows was also noted.

Lauderdale took advantage of the many opportunities to attend medical lectures at nearby Creighton University. Hospital duties kept Lauderdale busier than at any other time in his career. In January of 1896, he noted that the sick list for Fort Omaha was the highest in the department. He also made note of the "great number of cases of alcoholism in this command. Officers do not set [a] good example." The number of suicides resulting from alcoholism also concerned him. An outbreak of diphtheria in 1896 multiplied the workload on the hospital staff to near the breaking point. Lauderdale noted treating Lieutenant Humphrey, the quartermaster from Pine Ridge, during this outbreak.

Specific mention was made in journal entries of the thunderstorms, common to the Great Plains, that alarmed Joe. Curiously, there is no mention of her fear of these storms during their years at Fort Sully. Joe's sister Lizzie visited for an extended stay. On 19 July 1896 David Crockett Moore, the black cook, left the Lauderdale's employ, an event Lauderdale seemed to have no regrets over, although David had worked for him for almost twenty-four years.

At sixty-three years of age, Lauderdale's eyesight became a problem for the first time. He sought treatment from Dr. Gifford, a civilian doctor in Omaha.

During the presidential campaign of 1896 he attended a speech by William Jennings Bryant in his first of three tries for the White House. Lauderdale opposed Bryant's stand on the free coinage of silver, and presumably voted for McKinley.

The death of Dean Gardner on 10 August 1896 saddened Lauderdale. Gardner, whom Lauderdale had met on his trip to Pine Ridge, had become a close friend (see Lauderdale's letter of 1 January 1891). The Lauderdales attended Gardner's church during their tour in Omaha.

Fort Omaha began the process of closing in late 1896, moving the resources of the fort to nearby Fort Crook. Instead of moving, with so short a time before retirement, Lauderdale opted for leave. Packing their household

The Lauderdales in front of their quarters in Fort Omaha, 1896, from left to right John, Joe, Joe's sister Lizzy, Vance, Marjorie, and David Crockett Moore. Photograph courtesy of the Beinecke Rare Book and Manuscript Library, Yale University.

goods for shipment to New York, the entire family left for an extended vacation in the Denver area.

Among the highlights of their stay in Denver were the zoological gardens. The family wondered at such sights as the Garden of the Gods and the other breathtaking scenery of the Colorado Rockies. One item of special note, which delighted the children, was riding on a horse-drawn trolley. Upon reaching the top of a hill the driver would unhitch the horse and put the horse on a specially-designed platform in the trolley. The horse would then ride down the other side of the hill on the trolley, much to the delight of Marjorie and Vance.

Dr. Lauderdale retired from the army on 13 November 1896, his sixty-fourth birthday, and began a long and happy retirement. While waiting for their new house to be built in Brooklyn, the family vacationed for six months in Salt Lake City, San Diego, Los Angeles, Garden Grove, and San Francisco. Journal entries for this six-month period comment on old friends visited and places and events observed on the trip. Saltmaking near the Great Salt Lake, fascinated the children. The doctor suffered a tooth ache while in Salt Lake City and resorted to a little brandy two or three times a day for relief until a dentist could be located.

In August 1897 the Lauderdales moved into their new house at 241 84th Street in Brooklyn, New York. Here Lauderdale spent the remainder of his life. Special joy came from the thought that they could plant flowers in their new yard and live there long enough to enjoy them.

Correspondence slowed to a trickle and journal entries became less frequent during the next few years. With all the free time retirement offered, the Lauderdales' social and cultural activities increased. Lauderdale was able to join many fraternal organizations, including, the Sequoya League, the Society of Genesee (which was founded by the Indian Red Jacket), the YMCA, Empire State Society, Sons of the American Revolution, Art Society of Bay Ridge, the Military Service Institute, Crescent Athletic Club of Brooklyn, New York Academy of Science, and the Bellevue Hospital Alumni Society. He also became a member of the American Museum of Natural History.

Joe became an active member of the Brooklyn branch of the Suffrage Society, a national women's suffrage organization. Lauderdale left no record of his views on the movement to give women the vote. Joe also joined the Sorosis Club and enrolled as a member of the Hospital Auxiliary.[4] Both Joe and Lauderdale were active in their church, the New Brick Presbyterian. Trips were less common, although, in 1903 he traveled to Washington to visit the Old Soldiers Home, with a side trip to the Smithsonian Institution.

In 1903 Lauderdale's sister Frank became ill. He was closer to Frank than anyone else, with the exception of his wife. The vast majority of his letters over his career were to his favorite sister; they corresponded on a very regular basis and a bond developed between them that his marriage to Joe did not weaken. Joe and Frank, of course, were very close and were comfortable with their respective roles in Lauderdale's life. When illness struck his spinster sister, Lauderdale's letters to her took on a indelicate tone, absent in all of his previous correspondence. On 5 May 1903 he wrote her that her health problems were because she "had grown so stout . . . I think the slow heart rate must be due to excess of fat." He reported her heart rate good, her breathing shallow and rapid. Her heart could not return the blood from her extremities, however, causing her feet and ankles to swell. Lauderdale was in attendance when she died on 4 April, 1903. He kept his grief private and made no journal entries regarding her passing.

Attendance at the theater and other forms of cultural activities occupied much of the time remaining to Lauderdale and Joe. Joe passed away in 1913, after an illness of several months, leaving Lauderdale alone. Joe's death must have had a devastating effect on him, although there is nothing in his papers, save three small obituary notices and the LaFayette Ave. Presbyterian Church bulletin from 1915. The bulletin stated that the three sisters, Lizzie, Julia, and Carrie, donated flowers which graced the altar in memory of their late sister on the anniversary of her death. It was as if he wanted nothing to remind him of her passing.

The same year Joe died, Marjorie married Lt. Dean Hall, U.S. Army. In 1916 the Halls were living at Fort Grant in the Panama Canal Zone and Lauderdale enjoyed a visit with his daughter there. His interest naturally included the flora and fauna of the region and he derived great pleasure in seeing "The Big Ditch," as the canal was called. The engineering of the locks impressed him. His letters to Vance described the wonder and beauty of the Canal Zone.

Suffering from arteriosclerosis, John Vance Lauderdale, the oldest living retired officer of the U.S. Army, died on 22 January 1931, four decades after his tour at the Pine Ridge Reservation.

Notes

Chapter 1

1. Peter Josyph, *The Wounded River: The Civil War Letters of John Vance Lauderdale M.D.* (East Lansing: Michigan State University Press, 1993).
2. Letter from Lauderdale to the Army Medical Board, 3 December 1866, Record Group 94, L-174 Adustant General's Office [AGO] 1866, National Archives and Record Administration. (NARA), Washington D.C.
3. Alexander Hoff was the father of John Van R. Hoff, with whom Dr. Lauderdale served during his tour at Pine Ridge.
4. For an interesting account of the "Indian Ring" see George H. Phillips, "The Indian Ring in Dakota Territory, 1870-1890," *South Dakota History* 2, no. 1 (Fall 1972): 345-76.
5. *Annual Reports of the Surgeon General, 1870-90.*
6. Wesley Merritt, "The Army of the United States," *Harpers Monthly Magazine* 80, no. 478 (March 1890): 493-509.
7. Charles Lynch, Frank W. Weed, and Loy McAfee, *The Medical Department of the United States Army in the World War*, vol. 1 (Washington, D.C.: U.S. Government Printing Office, 1923).
8. Charles Smart, "First Aid to the Injured from the Army Standpoint, (Report of a paper read to the International Congress of Charities, Correction, and Philanthropy, Chicago Illinois) reprinted in *Medical Record* 44 (July 1893): 71-74.
9. Ibid.
10. Ibid.
11. Ibid.

12. Lynch, Weed, and McAfee, *The Medical Department of the United States Army*, 47.
13. Ibid.
14. Ibid.
15. *Annual Report of the Surgeon General of the Army*, 1888.
16. Ibid.
17. Ibid.
18. *House of Representatives Report Number 1405*, 47th cong., 1st sess.
19. *Annual Report of the Surgeon General*, 1884, quoted in *Senate Report No. 84*, Sen. doc. for the 49th cong., 1st sess.
20. *House of Representatives Report No. 3658*, 49th cong., 2d sess.
21. *New York Times*, 11 April 1912.
22. *Annual Report of the Surgeon General of the Army*, 1888.
23. P. M. Ashburn, *A History of the Medical Department of the United States Army* (Boston: Houghton Mifflin Co., 1929).
24. James Mooney, *The Ghost Dance Religion and the Sioux Outbreak of 1890* (Lincoln: University of Nebraska Press, 1991), 824.
25. Wilcomb E. Washburn, *The American Indian and the United States* (New York: Random House, 1973), 3: 2517, 2523, 2524.
26. Jerome A. Greene. "The Sioux Land Commission of 1889: A Prelude to Wounded Knee," *South Dakota History* 1 (Winter 1970): 41-72.
27. George Hyde, *A Sioux Chronicle* (Norman: University of Oklahoma Press, 1956), 232-33. Mooney, *The Ghost Dance*, 826.
28. This is based on an examination of rainfall data from various locations in and around the Lakota reservations that indicates the drought began in 1886 and did not end until the mid 1890s. Data for some locations is erratic, having not been reported in some months or years. It can be determined with relative certainty that rainfall on and around the reservations was down as much as 40 percent during the late 1880s and early 1890s. See James A. Ruffner, *Climates of the States* (Detroit: Gale Research Co., 1978), 2: 899, 904; John P. Finley, *Certain Climatic Features of the Two Dakotas* (Washington, D.C.: U.S. Government Printing Office, 1893); Cleophas C. O'Harra, *O'Harra's Handbook of the Black Hills* (Rapid City: The Black Hills Handbook Company, 1913). Hyde, *A Sioux Chronicle*, 176-77, 232-33.
29. *Annual Report of the Secretary of War* 1891, 133-34.
30. Bishop W. H. Hare, as quoted in Mooney, *The Ghost Dance*, 840.
31. *Annual Report of the Commissioner of Indian Affairs*, 1891, 1: 132-35.
32. *Annual Report of the Secretary of War*, 1891, 133-39.
33. Secretary of the Interior John Noble to the Commissioner of Indian Affairs[CIA], 6 December 1890, in "Reports and Correspondence Relating to the Army

Investigation of the Battle of Wounded Knee and to the Sioux Campaign of 1890-91," Microfilm publication number M-983 (hereafter cited as M-983), National Archives and Record Administration.

34. Miles to Schofield, 19 December 1890, M-983

35. Telegram from Brigadier General Thomas H. Ruger to AGO, 12 December 90, M-983.

36. Captain Joseph H. Hurst, quoted in Mooney, *The Ghost Dance*, 837.

37. Mooney, *The Ghost Dance*, 819-21.

38. Ibid.

39. Ibid.

40. Raymond J. DeMallie, "The Lakota Ghost Dance: An Ethnohistorical Account," *Pacific Historical Review* 51, no. 4 (1982): 388.

41. Mooney, *The Ghost Dance*, 819-24.

42. DeMallie, *The Lakota Ghost Dance*, 393-95.

43. Hyde, *A Sioux Chronicle*, 254.

44. CIA to Royer, 3 October 1890, M-983

45. Royer to CIA, 12 October 1890, M-983.

46. Charles Eastman, *From the Deep Woods to Civilization* (Lincoln: University of Nebraska Press, 1916), 93-95.

47. Palmer to CIA, 11 November 1890 and Royer to CIA, 12 November 1890, M-983.

48. Mooney, *The Ghost Dance*, 848.

49. Dr. V. T. McGillycuddy, quoted in Mooney, *The Ghost Dance*, 832; R. O. Pugh, quoted in Eli S. Ricker Collection, MS-8 (hereafter cited as MS-8), Nebraska State Historical Society.

50. R. O. Pugh, quoted in MS-8.

51. State of California Board of Medical Examiners to Robert Lee of the *Rapid City Journal*, 27 October 1953.

52. Commissioner of Indian Affairs to agents at Pine Ridge, Rosebud, Standing Rock, Cheyenne River, and Crow Creek Reservations, 20 November 1890, M-983.

53. Agents Reynolds, McLaughlin, and Dixon to Commissioner of Indian Affairs, 21 November 1890, M-983; Agent Palmer to CIA, 24 November 1890, M-983.

54. Royer to Commissioner of Indian Affairs, 26 November 1890, M-983.

55. Royer to Commissioner of Indian Affairs, 27 November 1890, M-983.

56. V. T. McGillycuddy, quoted in Mooney, *The Ghost Dance*, 831.

57. Oliver Knight, *Following the Indian Wars: The Story of the Newspaper Correspondents Among the Indian Campaigners* (Norman: University of Oklahoma Press, 1960), 311.

58. Elmo Scott Watson, "The Last Indian War, 1890-91—A Study of Newspaper Jingoism," *Journalism Quarterly* 20 (September 1943): 206.

59. Knight, *Following the Indian Wars*, 313.
60. Watson, "The Last Indian War", 205.
61. Knight, *Following the Indian Wars*, 314; Watson, "The Last Indian War", 212.
62. Watson, "The Last Indian War", 205.
63. *Annual Report of Commissioner of Indian Affairs*, 1891, 1: 132-35.
64. Miles to Brooke, 18 November 1890, M-983.
65. William H. Leckie, *The Buffalo Soldiers: A Narrative of the Negro Cavalry in the West* (Norman: University of Oklahoma Press, 1967), 26.
66. *Rapid City Daily Journal*, 10 December 1890, 1 and 11 December 1890: 1.
67. *Annual Report of the Surgeon General of the Army*, 1891, 599.
68. Morgan quoted in Mooney, *The Ghost Dance*, 852.
69. Lieutenant Colonel A. T. Smith to AGO, 26 November 1890, M-983.
70. George W. Baird, "General Miles' Indian Campaigns," *Century Magazine* 42 (July 1891): 351-70.
71. Virginia W. Johnson, *The Unregimented General: A Biography of Nelson A. Miles* (Boston: Houghton Mifflin Co., 1962), 282; *Annual Report of the Secretary of War*, 1891, 134-40.
72. *Annual Report of the Secretary of War*, 1891, 147-48.
73. Ibid.
74. Miles to AGO, 27 December 1890 and 1 January 1891, M-983
75. Mooney, *The Ghost Dance*, 862.
76. Stanley Vestal, *Sitting: Bull Champion of the Sioux* (Norman: University of Oklahoma Press, 1932), 271-72; Robert Utley, *The Lance and the Shield: The Life and Times of Sitting Bull* (New York: Henry Holt Co., 1993), 285.
77. Dewey Beard quoted in MS-8.
78. Beard and Joseph Horn Cloud quoted in MS-8.
79. Beard quoted in MS-8; Andrew Good Thunder quoted in Walter Mason Camp Collection (Field Notes and Interviews, Box 6, Folder 4, Envelope 90), Lilly Library, Indiana University.
80. Beard and Horn Cloud quoted in MS-8; Good Thunder quoted in Camp Collection (Field Notes and Interviews, Box 6, Folder 4, Envelope 90).
81. Ibid.
82. These figures were compiled from the "Returns From Regiments for the Seventh U.S. Cavalry and the First U.S. Infantry," December 1890, M-744, Record Group 94, National Archives and Record Administration. These figures do not include teamsters, traders, ambulance drivers, or reporters who are known to have been present. Had these men been included the number of armed white men would well exceed 500.

83. Colonel James Forsyth's official report, M-983

84. Miles to AGO, 18 November 1891, Miles Papers, United States Army Military History Institute, Carlisle Barracks, Carlisle, Pennsylvania.

85. Ibid.

86. Forsyth to Assistant Adjutant General [AAG] Department of the Platte, 31 December 1890, M-983

87. Charles B. Ewing, "The Wounds of the Wounded Knee Battle Field, with Remarks on Wounds Produced by Large and Small Caliber Bullets," Transactions of the Second Annual Meeting of the Association of Military Surgeons of the National Guard of the United States (April 1892): 36-56.

88. Richard Jensen, "Big Foot's Followers at Wounded Knee," *Nebraska History* 71, no. 4 (Winter 1990): 194-212. This number includes all males between the ages of 17 and 50, from lists a, b, h, p, q, t, u, v, z, bb, g, i, ff, gg, and hh.

89. Francis J. Ives, "Personal Diary," Robinson Museum, South Dakota Historical Society, H-84.38. Ives treated thirty-five wounded Lakota. Of those, seventeen suffered multiple gunshot wounds. There were also a total of six with compound fractures; one had two compound fractures. Several had both multiple gunshot wounds and compound fractures. These figures do not include any Indians who were wounded and fled or rescued by relatives before the soldiers could capture them.

90. Paddy Starr, Beard, and Horn Cloud quoted in MS-8.

91. Gilbert Bailey, quoted in the Walter Mason Camp Collection, MSS 57, Harold B. Lee Library, Brigham Young University.

92. Ewing, quoted in Kent-Baldwin Investigation of the Battle of Wounded Knee, M-983.

93. Miles to G. W. Baird, 20 November 1891, MSS WA-S901, M596, The Western Americana Collection, The Beinecke Rare Book and Manuscript Library, Yale University.

94. Ewing, quoted in Kent-Baldwin, M-983.

95. Ibid.

96. Miles to AGO, 1 January 1891, M-983.

97. Miles to AGO, 9 February 1891, Miles Papers, United States Army Military History Institute.

98. Royer to CIA, 31 December 1890, M-983, Ives' Diary.

99. John R. Brooke to AAG, 25 January 1891, M-983.

100. Statement of the Rev. Mr. Cook, 26 January 1891, M-983.

101. Forsyth to Brooke 30 January 1891, Miles to AGO 4 February 1891-M983.

102. Valentine T. McGillycuddy, quoted in the Walter Mason Camp Field Notes, Unclassified Envelope #4, Little Big Horn National Battlefield Archives. Peter McFarland quoted in MS-8 discusses scalping of dead Indians at Wounded Knee.

103. Mooney, *The Ghost Dance*, 888.

104. Miles to Forsyth, Special Orders, No. 8, M-983.

105. Robert H. Steiback, *A Long March: The Lives of Frank and Alice Baldwin* (Austin: University of Texas Press, 1981), 158.

106. Peter R. DeMontravel, "General Nelson A. Miles and the Wounded Knee Controversy," *Arizona and the West* 28, no. 1 (Spring 1986): 23-44.

107. Mrs. Alice Baldwin to Brininstool, 20 October 1926, Earl A. Brininstool Papers, MSS 1412, Lee Library, Brigham Young University.

108. Miles to Baird, 10 November 1891, MSS WA-5901, M596, The Western American Collection, The Beinecke Rare Book and Manuscript Library, Yale University

109. General Orders No. 100 AGO, 17 December 1891. Also see Jerry Green, "The Medals of Wounded Knee," *Nebraska History* 75, no. 2 (Summer 1994): 200-208.

110. William J. Ghent, "The Seventh Regiment of United States Cavalry," Edward S. Godfrey Papers, Library of Congress. This manuscript was initially drafted by E. A. Garlington ca. 1894. L. S. McCormick edited the text ca. 1904. E. S. Godfrey made minor revisions in the 1930s. It was then published by Ghent.

111. Mooney, *The Ghost Dance*, 889-90; Kent to AAG, 25 January 1891 and Pierce to AAG, 21 February 1891 and 24 February 1891, M-983.

112. Ibid.

113. Ibid.

114. *Annual Report of the Secretary of War*, 1891.

115. Miles to AGO, 18 November 1891, Miles Papers United States Army Military History Institute.

116. James C. Olson. *Redcloud and the Sioux Problem* (Lincoln: University of Nebraska Press, 1965), 333.

117. *Annual Report of the Secretary of War*, 1891.

118. Ibid.

119. Miles telegram to AGO, 25 February 1891, M-983.

120. Robert M. Utley. "The Ordeal of Plenty Horses," *American Heritage* 26, no. 1 (December 1974): 15-86.

Chapter 2

1. Lauderdale is referring to the massacre at Wounded Knee Creek on 29 December 1890.

2. Marshall, Michigan.

3. Julia Lane, Lauderdale's sister-in-law, who came to stay with his wife during his absence.

4. Thomas J. Morgan, Commissioner of Indian Affairs.

5. William H. Hare, Episcopal missionary. Bishop Hare served as the first Episcopalian missionary bishop to the Indians.

6. Captain George Ruhlen, assistant quartermaster.

7. Captain Charles Frederic Humphrey.

8. Valentine T. McGillycuddy, a medical doctor who served as Indian agent at Pine Ridge from 1879 to 1886. McGillycuddy was en route to Pine Ridge, in his capacity as Assistant Adjutant General of South Dakota, to determine the extent of danger to settlers in the surrounding areas.

9. Captain Myles Moylan, commanding officer of Troop A Seventh Cavalry.

10. Troop A under Moylan lost six killed and four wounded in the Wounded Knee Massacre. This represents approximately 17 percent of the army casualties from the encounter.

11. Lieutenant John Skinner Mallory.

12. Brigader General John R. Brooke, commanding officer, Department of the Platte.

13. Major General Nelson A. Miles, commander, division of the Missouri.

14. Captain Frank and Mrs. Alice Baldwin. Captain Baldwin, of the Fifth Infantry, was a member of Miles' staff and was later appointed to the board of inquiry investigating Colonel Forsyth's conduct at the Wounded Knee Massacre.

15. First Lieutenant Ernest A. Garlington, Troop A Seventh Cavalry. Garlington was wounded in the elbow during the Wounded Knee Massacre.

16. Reverend Charles S. Cook, a mixed-blood Yankton Sioux who was the Episcopal Missionary at Pine Ridge. Rev. Cook allowed the use of his church for the care of the Lakotas wounded during the Wounded Knee Massacre.

17. The reporters covering the "uprising" on the Great Sioux Reservation in 1890-91, because of the lack of real news, earned the reputation of making up stories to keep their editors happy. For further detail see Oliver Knight, *Following the Indian Wars: The Story of Newspaper Correspondents Among Indian Campaigners* (Norman: University of Oklahoma Press, 1960); Watson, "The Last Indian War," 205-19.

18. Captain Allyn Capron, commanding officer, First Artillery. The destructive work he mentions was done with a battery of four Hotchkiss mountain guns (or cannons). These guns fired up to fifty, 2-pound 10-ounce explosive shells per minute. Many Lakota women and children were killed and wounded by the fire from these weapons.

19. First Lieutenant Ezra B. Fuller, quartermaster, Seventh Cavalry.

20. Captain and Assistant Surgeon Charles B. Ewing.

21. Captain and Assistant Surgeon Francis J. Ives. Captain Ives was assigned primary responsibility for treating the wounded Indian prisoners held in the Episcopal

Church. He kept a diary detailing the wounds suffered by those Lakota prisoners brought to the agency at Pine Ridge for treatment of their wounds.

22. This was probably an unnamed one-year-old male child listed as number 18 in Ives' diary. The child had multiple gunshot wounds to the buttocks and scrotum. He was transferred to the Indian camp on 9 January 1891.

23. Doctor Charles A. Eastman, a full-blooded Santee Sioux.

24. These figures have been proven to fall short of the actual number of Lakota killed at Wounded Knee. A more realistic figure would be 260. See: Jensen "Big Foot's Followers at Wounded Knee," 194-212.

25. This soldier was Private Harry L. Duncan, Troop A Seventh Cavalry, wounded at the Wounded Knee Massacre.

26. Captain and Assistant Surgeon Robert J. Gibson.

27. Miss Elaine Goodale, a missionary and school teacher. At this time she had been in the Dakotas working with the Lakotas for several years.

28. Lieutenant Colonel Dallas Bache, medical director for the army that was brought together in the winter of 1890-91.

29. Lieutenant Colonel Charles R. Greenleaf, assistant medical purveyor of the U.S. Army.

30. Captain and Assistant Surgeon John Oscar Skinner.

31. Colonel William R. Shafter, commanding officer, First Infantry.

32. The presence of guards around the school was another reason for discontent among the Lakota people. Many Lakotas believed that their children were being held hostage, thus preventing them from fleeing the reservation. This of course was denied by the authorities.

33. Agent Daniel F. Royer.

34. Susette LaFlesche Tibbles, wife of Thomas Tibbles, a reporter for the *Omaha World-Herald*.

35. Major and Surgeon William Henry Gardner. There were two Dr. Gardners at Pine Ridge during this time, the major mentioned above, who had a drinking problem, and Captain Edwin F. Gardner (see note 81).

36. Colonel Albert Gallatin Brackett.

37. Captain and Assistant Surgeon Henry Sayles Kilborne.

38. Lieutenant E. W. Casey, Twenty-second Infantry, commanding officer of the Cheyenne scouts. He was killed by Plenty Horses, a young Brule warrior, near White Clay Creek.

39. For an interesting account of the friction between the Interior and War Departments, see Robert Wooster, *The Military and United States Indian Policy 1865-1903* (New Haven: Yale University Press, 1988).

40. In addition to the units listed by Dr. Lauderdale (no record can be found of the 16th Infty being in the area), the Nebraska National Guard under the command of General L. W. Colby was called to active duty to protect the settlers in nearby Nebraska. Governor Arthur C. Mellette of South Dakota also armed local civilians with arms supplied by the federal government.

41. General Miles' plan was to encircle the "hostile" Lakotas with his troops, slowly pushing them to the agency at Pine Ridge. This plan would, he hoped, settle the "uprising" peacefully. The plan was working prior to Colonel Forsyth's blunder at Wounded Knee Creek.

42. Father Francis Craft, a Catholic missionary assigned to the Holy Rosary Mission. Father Craft was present at Wounded Knee Creek and suffered a knife wound in the affair.

43. Captain Francis Edwin Pierce was appointed Indian agent for Pine Ridge Reservation by General Miles.

44. Captain Ezra P. Ewers.

45. Captain William E. Dougherty.

46. During this time the troops were fortifying their positions in and around the agency proper, not knowing if the Lakota might attack.

47. The Indian boarding school in Carlisle, Pennsylvania, founded by Captain Richard H. Pratt.

48. Indian boarding schools at Carlisle, Pennsylvania and Hampton, Virginia.

49. A search of Lauderdale's papers found no evidence that he ever wrote of his life and times.

50. Phillip Wells, a mixed-blood scout and interpreter serving the U.S. Army.

51. Lauderdale is mockingly referring to the Messiah, or Wovoka, who originated the Ghost Dance or, as it was sometimes called, the Messiah Craze.

52. The two soldiers who died were Privates Harry B. Stone, Troop B Seventh Cavalry, and George Elliott, Troop K Seventh Cavalry. Both men suffered large caliber gunshot wounds. Elliott's leg was so badly damaged by bullet wounds that it had to be amputated 4" below the knee by Dr. Ewing. Infection set in and he died. Stone suffered four gunshot wounds; one of the bullets removed weighed 385 grains. These types of wounds further serve to prove the theory that many soldiers were caught in a crossfire with other troops. The Indians did not possess the large caliber weapon used to inflict such wounds. See Ewing, "The Wounds of the Wounded Knee Battle Field."

53. Lieutenant and Assistant Surgeon William H. Bowan.

54. Major and Surgeon Leonard Wood.

55. Captain and Assistant Surgeon William Gardner Spencer.

56. Captain and Assistant Surgeon John James Kane.

57. Captain and Assistant Surgeon Daniel M. Appel.

58. Major and Surgeon Albert Hartstuff.

59. Captain and Assistant Surgeon Edward Perry Vollum.

60. Lauderdale is referring to the birth of his brother Willis' grandson.

61. Lady was one of the Lauderdale family's horses.

62. Captain and Assistant Surgeon John Van R. Hoff. Dr. Hoff was the son of Doctor Alexander Hoff, commanding officer of the *D. A. January*, the hospital ship on which Lauderdale served during the Civil War. The younger Dr. Hoff was instrumental in organizing the army's field hospital, and Hospital Corps.

63. Young Man Afraid of his Horses, a highly-respected Oglala chief. Young Man Afraid was instrumental in the peace movement among the Lakota.

64. The officers in this photo have been identified by other sources. These identifications do not agree with Lauderdale's, however. Where Lauderdale mentions Lieutenants. Sims and Markham, others identify these men as George W. Kirkman and Frank O. Ferris.

65. W. R. Cross. Cross was living in Hot Springs, South Dakota at this time.

66. This Lakota woman was Mrs. Few Tails, who had accompanied her husband, along with One Feather, his wife, and their two children, on a hunting trip to the Black Hills. While returning to their reservation, they were the victims of an unprovoked attack by a party of white men.

67. Captain and assistant surgeon George Milton Wells.

68. Captain Pierce, the acting Indian agent, requested Colonel Shafter to send a guard detachment to break up the reported gambling on the reservation. The guards confiscated two boxes of gambling equipment, including at least one box of faro tools. The owner, B. F. Stetson of Rushville, offered Captain Pierce a bribe of "$50 or $75" for their return. See Miscellaneous Correspondence, Box 31, Pine Ridge Records, National Archives and Record Administration, Regional Records Center, Kansas City, MO.

69. Colonel Robert Hilton Offley.

70. Teresa Howard Dean, *Chicago Herald* correspondent. Mrs. Dean is acknowledged as the first female war correspondent, even though she did not arrive at Pine Ridge until the hostilities had ended.

71. Colonel Guy V. Henry, commanding officer of the Ninth Cavalry.

72. David Crockett Moore, the Lauderdales' black cook, who had worked for Lauderdale since September 1872.

73. First Lieutenant John Loomis Chamberlin.

74. Colonel James W. Forsyth, commanding officer of the Seventh Cavalry. Forsyth was in command of the army forces at Wounded Knee Creek 29 December 1890.

Lauderdale refers to him as general because, like many other officers who served during the Civil War, Forsyth was promoted to the rank of brigidier general of volunteers. After the war, those officers who remained in the regular army reverted to their former rank. The title general was honorary.

75. General Miles relieved Forsyth of his command because of the high number of noncombatant deaths and the large number of army casualties as a result of crossfire at Wounded Knee.

76. Colonel Eugene A. Carr, commanding officer, Sixth Cavalry.

77. Colonel Frank Wheaton, commanding officer, Second Infantry.

78. Lieutenant Charles W. Taylor, Ninth Cavalry.

79. Captain and Assistant Surgeon Julian Mayo Cabell.

80. Lieutenant John Stafford.

81. Captain and Assistant Surgeon Edwin F. Gardner.

82. Captain and Assistant Surgeon James L. Powell, the Lauderdales' neighbor at Fort Ontario.

83. Captain and Assistant Surgeon Charles Moore Gandy.

84. General Charles Sutherland, surgeon general of the army.

85. Lieutenant and Assistant Surgeon Alfred E. Bradley.

86. Mrs. James F. Asay, wife of one of the Indian traders.

87. The actual number of Lakota leaders General Miles took to be held as prisoners at Fort Sheridan, Illinios was twenty-five. This was to ensure the cooperation of those Lakotas remaining on the reservation.

88. Captain Robert G. Armstrong, First U.S. Infantry.

89. Participants in the Sun Dance, the most sacred of the Lakota rituals, had sticks thrust through their flesh. Their chest and/or back was pierced with a wooden skewer and pressure was then placed on it until the flesh tore or was cut free. The pressure came from being suspended from the Sun Dance pole or having buffalo skulls tied to the skewers. For a detailed account of the Sun Dance see Frances Densmore, *Teton Sioux Music and Culture* (Lincoln: University of Nebraska Press, 1992); James R. Walker, *Lakota Belief and Ritual* (Lincoln: University of Nebraska Press, 1980); Joseph Epps Brown, *The Sacred Pipe: Black Elks Account of the Seven Rites of the Oglala Sioux* (Norman: University of Oklahoma Press, 1953).

90. No record could be found that Red Nest had ever enlisted in the scout service for the U.S. Army. He did collect payment from the government for property destroyed during the unrest on the reservation.

91. Walter E. Lauderdale, Lauderdale's younger brother.

92. This clipping was of the newspaper article entitled "Teresa and Big Injun," by Teresa Dean. Which appeared in the *Chicago Herald*, 20 January 1891.

93. According to the official report, no officer was killed in the train accident of 26 January 1891, which involved the Seventh Cavalry. Two enlisted men, Sergeant Chantilly and Private Meil, were killed. Captains Godfrey and Ilsley, along with fifteen enlisted men, were injured.

94. *Army and Navy Journal.*

95. Preston B. Plumb, republican senator from Kansas, 1877-1891.

96. Captain and Assistant Surgeon Fred Crayton Ainsworth.

97. All reports from both military officials and Indian agents called for an increase in rations for the people on the reservation. These reports all show a severe shortage of food and supplies to all agencies, caused in part by congressional inaction on Indian appropriations bills and theft by many agents of the government in charge of providing goods and services to the reservations. See statements from Commissioner Morgan, ex-Agent McGillycuddy, General Miles, Captain Hurst, and Bishop Hare (quoted in Mooney, *The Ghost Dance*, 829-42). See also *Annual Report of the Secretary of War,* 1891.

98. The overcoat described by Lauderdale was adopted in October 1883 by the quartermaster general.

99. Lieutenant Colonel James S. Casey, First Infantry.

100. Lieutenant Louis Harvie Strothers.

101. Lieutenant Robert Nelson Getty.

102. Captain Charles George Penny.

103. Dyspepsia was the term used to describe chronic gastrointestinal problems, what is now termed acid indigestion or heartburn.

104. Mildred was the daughter of the Lauderdales' neighbors, Captain and Mrs. Powell.

105. Lieutenant George Henry Sands.

106. First Lieutenant Charles Grenville Starr.

107. Reverend Amos Ross.

108. Second Lieutenant Frank Long Winn.

109. Lieutenant John Stanford Mason, Jr.

110. General Edward O. C. Ord.

111. Major Thaddeus Harlan Stanton.

112. No such picture could be found in the Lauderdale collection.

113. Private William J. Davis, Troop K Seventh U.S. Cavalry. Davis recovered from his wounds and was discharged on 4 June 1891, at Fort Riley, Kansas.

114. Captain and Assistant Surgeon William P. Kendall.

115. Plenty Horses was held at Fort Mead until his trial in Sioux Falls, South Dakota, in April 1891.

116. Colonel James Forsyth was exonerated of any wrongdoing in the massacre at Wounded Knee Creek, due in part to political pressure exerted on the officers comprising the board of inquiry. General Miles was infuriated and saw the exoneration as a personal affront.

117. These Lakota leaders were among those who went to Washington to meet with government officials. The meetings were held as an attempt to alleviate some of the problems that caused the dissatisfaction that brought the army to the reservations.

118. Reverend William Cleveland.

119. George Sword was the captain of the Indian police force on Pine Ridge.

120. This was the statement of Mrs. Few Tails regarding the attack on the party of Lakota returning to the reservation from a hunt. See letter dated 24 February 1891, Captain F. E. Pierce to AAG, Division of the Missouri, M-983.

121. Census agent A. T. Lea. Perhaps Lea's lack of attention to his duties explains the wide variations in the population counts of the Lakota on the reservations during this period. Agent Wright at the Rosebud Reservation had been instructed "to pay no attention to Lea's count" on 1 June 1890. See the Lebbeus F. Spencer Collection, MS-596, State Historical Society of Colorado, Denver, CO.

122. Mrs. James A. Finlay, wife of one of the Indian traders and innkeeper on the Pine Ridge Reservation.

Chapter 3

1. Colson E. Warne, *The Pullman Boycott of 1894: The Problem of Federal Intervention* (Boston: Heath Co., 1955); Leon Stein, *The Pullman Strike* (New York: Arno Press, 1969).

2. McAlister Coleman, *Eugene V. Debs: A Man Unafraid* (Westport: Hyperion Press, 1975).

3. *The Junction City Union* [Kansas], 7 November 1891.

4. John W. Leonard, *Women's Who's Who of America* (Detroit: Gale Research Co., 1976), 477.

Bibliography

Documents

Beinecke Rare Book and Manuscript Library, Western Americana Collection,
    Yale University:
George W. Baird Collection, MSS WA-S901, M596.
John Vance Lauderdale Collection, MSS WA-S1319.
James W. Forsyth Collection, MSS WA-S1404.

Harold B. Lee Library, Brigham Young University:
Earl A. Brininstool Papers, MSS 1412.
Walter Mason Camp Collection, MSS 57.

Lilly Library, Indiana University:
Walter Mason Camp Collection.

Library of Congress:
Edward S. Godfrey Papers.

Little Big Horn National Battlefield Archives:
Walter Mason Camp Field Notes.

Nebraska State Historical Society:
Eli S. Ricker Collection, MS-8.

South Dakota State Historical Society:
Francis J. Ives Personal Diary. H-84.38.

United States Army Military History Institute:
Nelson A. Miles Papers.

State Historical Society of Colorado:
Lebbeus F. Spencer Collection, MS-596.

Robert Lee, letter From California State Board of Medical Examiners, 27
     October 1953.
Charles Smart, Report of a paper read to the International Congress of
Charities, Correction, and Philanthropy, Chicago, Illinois, 1893.

Government Documents

Annual Report of the Commissioner of Indian Affairs, 1891.Washington D.C.:
     U.S. Government and Printing Office, 1892.

Annual Report of the Secretary of War, 1891. 1 Washington D.C.:
     U.S. Government Printing Office, 1892.

Annual Report of the Surgeon General of the Army, 1870-1890. Washington
     D.C.: U.S. Government Printing Office, 1871-91.

Annual Report of the Surgeon General of the Army, 1891. Washington D.C.:
     U.S. Government Printing Office, 1892.

National Archives and Record Administration Record Group 94
"Returns from Regiments." M-744.
"Enlistment Records." M-233.
"Adjutant General's Office [AGO] Letters Received." 1368 Appointments,
     Commissions, and Personal [ACP] 1891.

"AGO Letters Received. "16045 Primary Record Division [PRD] 1891.
"AGO Letters Received." L-174 PRD 1866.
"AGO General Orders No. 100." 17 December 1891.
"Reports and Correspondence Relating to the Army Investigation of the
    Battle of Wounded Knee and to the Sioux Campaign of 1890-1891."
    Microfilm Publication M-983.

Miscellaneous Correspondence, Box 31, Pine Ridge Record. National
    Archives and Record Administration, Regional Records Center, Kansas
    City, MO.

47th Congress. 1st Session. House Document 1405.
49th Congress. 1st Session. Senate Document 84.
49th Congress. 2nd Session. House Document 3658.

Books

Ashburn, Percy M. *A History of the Medical Department of the United States
    Army*. Boston: Houghton Mifflin Co., 1929.
Brown, Joseph E. *The Sacred Pipe Black Elks Account of the Seven Rites of
    the Oglala Sioux*. Norman: University of Oklahoma Press, 1953.
Coleman, McAlister. *Eugene V. Debs: A Man Unafraid*. Westport: Hyperion
    Press, 1975.
Densmore, Frances *Teton Sioux Music and Culture*. Lincoln: University of
    Nebraska Press, 1992
Eastman, Charles A. *From the Deep Woods to Civilization*. Lincoln:
    University of Nebraska Press, 1916.
Finley, John P. *Certain Climatic Features of the Two Dakotas*. Washington,
    D.C.: U.S. Government Printing Office, 1893.
Hyde, George E. *A Sioux Chronicle*. Norman: University of Oklahoma Press,
    1956.
Johnson, V. W. *The Unregimented General: A Biography of Nelson A. Miles*.
    Boston: Houghton Mifflin Co., 1962.
Josyph, Peter. *The Wounded River: The Civil War Letters of John Vance
    Lauderdale, M.D.* East Lansing: Michigan State University Press, 1993.

Knight, Oliver. *Following the Indian Wars: The Story of the Newspaper Correspondents Among Indian Campaigners.* Norman: University of Oklahoma Press, 1960.

Leckie, William H. *The Buffalo Soldiers: A Narrative of the Negro Cavalry in the West.* Norman: University of Oklahoma Press, 1967.

Leonard, John W. *Women's Who's Who of America.* Detroit: Gale Research Co., 1976.

Lynch, Charles, Frank W. Weed, and Loy McAfee. *The Medical Department of the United States Army in the World War.* Washington, D.C.: Government Printing Office, 1923.

Mooney, James. *The Ghost Dance Religion and the Sioux Outbreak of 1890.* Lincoln: University of Nebraska Press, 1991.

O'Harra, Cleophas C. *O'Harra's Handbook of the Black Hills.* Rapid City: The Black Hills Handbook Company, 1913.

Olson, James D. *Red Cloud and the Sioux Problem.* Lincoln: University of Nebraska Press, 1965.

Ruffner, James A. *Climates of the States Volume 2.* Detroit: Gale Research Co., 1978.

Stein, Leon. *The Pullman Strike.* New York: Arno, 1969.

Steinback, R. H. *A Long March: The Lives of Frank and Alice Baldwin.* Austin: University of Texas Press, 1989.

Utley, Robert. *The Lance and the Shield: The Life and Times of Sitting Bull.* New York: Henry Holt Co., 1993.

Vestal, Stanley. *Sitting Bull, Champion of the Sioux.* Norman: University of Oklahoma Press, 1932.

Walker, James R. *Lakota Belief and Ritual.* Lincoln: University of Nebraska Press, 1980.

Waren, Colston E. *The Pullman Boycott of 1894: The Problem of Federal Intervention.* Boston: Heath, 1955.

Washburn, W. E. *The American Indian and the United States: A Documentary History.* New York: Random House, 1973.

Wooster, Robert. *Nelson A. Miles and the Twilight of the Frontier Army.* Lincoln: University of Nebraska Press, 1993.

Wooster, Robert. *The Military and United States Indian Policy, 1865-1903.* New Haven: Yale University Press, 1988.

Articles

Baird, George W. "General Miles' Indian Campaigns." *Century Magazine* 42 (1934): 351-70.

DeMallie Raymond J. "The Lakota Ghost Dance: An Ethnohistorical Account." *Pacific History Review* 51, no. 4 (November 1982): 385-405.

DeMontravel, P. R. "General Nelson A. Miles and the Wounded Knee Controversy." *Arizona and the West* 28 (spring 1986): 23-44.

Ewing, Charles B. "The Wounds of the Wounded Knee Battle Field, With Remarks on Wounds Produced by Large and Small Caliber Bullets." *Transactions of the Second Annual Meeting of the Association of Military Surgeons of the National Guard of the United States*, (April 1892): 36-56.

Green, Jerry. "The Medals of Wounded Knee." *Nebraska History* 75, no. 2 (Summer 1994): 200-208.

Greene Jerome A. "The Sioux Land Commission of 1889: A Prelude to Wounded Knee." *South Dakota History* 1 (Winter 1970): 41-72.

Jensen Richard E. "Big Foot's Followers at Wounded Knee." *Nebraska History* 71 (Fall 1990): 194-212.

Merritt, Wesley, "The Army of the United States," *Harpers Monthly Magazine* 80, no. 478 (March 1090). 493-509.

Phillips, George H. "The Indian Ring in Dakota Territory 1870-1890." *South Dakota History* 2 (fFall 1972): 344-76.

Smart, Charles. "First Aid to the Injured from the Army Standpoint." *Medical Record* 44 (July 1893): 71-74.

Utley, Robert M. "The Ordeal of Plenty Horses." *American Heritage* 26, no. 1 (December 1974): 15-86.

Watson, Elmo Scott. "The Last Indian War, 1890-1891—A Study of Newspaper Jingoism." *Journalism Quarterly* 20, no. 5 (1943): 205-19.

Newspapers

Chicago Herald, 20 January 1891.

Junction City Union [Kansas], 7 November 1891.

New York Times, 11 April 1912.

Rapid City Daily Journal, 10, 11 December 1891.

Index

177